AF431369

The Colors of my Life

ACTION, ADVENTURE & A LIFE PACKED WITH PURPOSE

PEGGY WOODS

innovo PUBLISHING
innovopublishing.com

Published by Innovo Publishing, LLC
www.innovopublishing.com
1-888-546-2111

Innovo Publishing LLC is a Christ-centered publisher located near Memphis, TN. Since 2008, Innovo has published quality books, eBooks, audiobooks, music, screenplays, and online and physical curricula that support the Great Commission, equip believers, and help create a positive Christian worldview. Innovo's capabilities and global reach provide Christian authors, artists, and ministries access to the world for Christ. To learn more about Innovo Publishing, visit our website at innovopublishing.com. To connect with other Christian creatives and to learn best practices for creating, publishing, marketing, and selling Christian titles, visit the Christian Publishing Portal at cpportal.com.

THE COLORS OF MY LIFE
Action, Adventure & a Life Packed with Purpose

ISBN: 979-8-88928-090-3

Cover Design & Interior Layout: Innovo Publishing, LLC

Printed in the United States of America
U.S. Printing History
First Edition: 2025

Acknowledgments

Thanks to my motivator, Kristy Shelton; my writing helpers, Pat Smith, Norma Brock, and Sue Lawrence; and my daughter, Bekah Brewer, for finishing the project. I thank Dr. Bart Dahmer and Innovo Publishing for their work helping me put this together. And I thank God for His presence and guidance in my life.

Contents

Introduction

I am a member of what some may call the *greatest generation of our time*. The hallmark of my generation is that we came of age during the Great Depression, and a vast majority of us either fought or supported the troops at home during WWII. We were known for our resilience; we had no choice but to adapt and move on. We had to make extraordinary changes in our daily lives because of extreme economic, social, technological, and cultural revolutions in our rapidly changing world. As I write this, I am nearly one hundred years old. I'm proud that I have lived a very full, interesting life, and I want to share some of my memories with you.

Since retiring, I've had occasions to share my life story at professional meetings and spiritual women's retreats. Many of my friends have suggested I write about my experiences. As time passed, I thought this might be a good idea. I wanted to do it especially for my wonderful family but also so that I had a fun project to keep me busy. It would allow me to tell some of the stories I've never told in the full context of my life. Some of my stories are about truly unique experiences, and some are as old as time but are told from my way of seeing things.

Like many little girls, I had big dreams growing up. I imagined a glamorous fashion job, a good marriage and children, and a wonderful life full of Christian joy and love. At the same time, something was always pulling me toward dreams of excitement and adventure.

In 1944, while in college, I was presented with an opportunity that would give me the experience of a lifetime. In a world mired in war, poverty, and discontent, fortune smiled on me. I felt I should do my duty since all the boys my age were being drafted or volunteering for service. The entire culture of the time was war focused; my father volunteered for the Draft Board, and even my community's Girl Scout troop got involved in the war effort.

I worked for the Office of Strategic Services—the OSS. It was the newly formed, top-secret project of the United States government. Founded after Congress declared war (after Japan's bombing of our air base in Pearl Harbor, Hawaii, on December 7th, 1941), the OSS was America's first independent intelligence agency. It was established to coordinate covert activities behind enemy lines for all our military branches, and it performed both clandestine paramilitary as well as intelligence-gathering operations. The OSS was formally disbanded on September 20th, 1945, after World War II ended, but it formed the basis for what is now our nation's Central Intelligence Agency (CIA) and Special Forces units.

After fifty years, WWII files were finally opened and the secrets of the OSS made public. Since then, numerous books about the OSS have been written, and I've learned so much more—the curtain has been pulled back on my hush-hush wartime job. Now I understand specific details concerning my *oh-so-secret* work, and I'm grateful for this new information. It helps put my OSS experiences into context.

Stories surface now as the solitude of silence reminds me of memories stored away long ago. I very much enjoy recalling these past events, reliving them in my mind and writing them down for those interested. My purpose in telling these stories is to share the important events of the time from my perspective.

These are some of my memorable stories—both personal and professional—that may give you a glimpse of life in the South, spanning from the 1920s until now, ninety-nine years later. I hope you enjoy them.

CHAPTER 1

Duty Called,
So I Answered

It was May 1944, and the world was floundering in chaos. I was a sophomore at Alabama College, State College for Women in Montevallo, Alabama, a liberal arts school established to teach women to be self-sufficient in a time when most are not. I was enrolled there as an art major. I boarded a bus headed to Montgomery, the capital of Alabama, to apply for a summer job with the Social Security Administration. I was on a mission.

With World War II in full force, posters were plastered on storefronts in every city and town—they were everywhere. Many featured pictures of Uncle Sam pointing a finger with the caption, "Uncle Sam Wants YOU for the US Army!" "Rosie the Riveter" was flexing her muscle, encouraging women to get out and work, with the slogan, "We Can Do It!" Women were joining the workforce for the first time, stepping up across the country to work on assembly lines or wherever they were needed. Making history, working for victory!

All Americans were urged to buy war bonds, join the war services, or volunteer to help with the war effort. I knew so many of the boys in my town's high school senior class and in my own neighborhood who had already volunteered for duty or been drafted. Many had dropped out of school to volunteer for duty rather than face the draft. My daddy was the volunteer chairman of the Draft Board, and he knew all about the boys being drafted.

There was scarcely any part of the world that hadn't been drawn into the war effort. Even Princess Elizabeth joined Britain's Auxiliary Territorial Service (ATS) as soon as she turned eighteen, and she drove and maintained military vehicles for her country. In Montevallo, the Girl Scouts were "Knittin' for Britain" long before the United States joined the Allied Forces on December 8th, 1941—the day after Japan bombed our naval air base in Pearl Harbor, Hawaii.

There was an entire culture shift happening then—women going to work, young men preparing to go to war, volunteers coming out of the woodwork. Most people were eager to do their part. In all this patriotic war culture, it was easy to be swept up, and my sense of patriotism led me to a decision: I was going to apply for a civil service position. Since I was already working and attending college, I figured part-time as a civil service clerk would be a perfect summer job. How could I do any less? My sense of duty was strong; I wanted to do my part. I was confident I could serve my country, even though the boys would be the ones actually fighting overseas.

Uncle Zed Mahan met me in Montgomery when I got off the bus. He had happily arranged for me to take the civil service exam, which would take place at the recreation center where Uncle Zed had responsibilities and helped out as he could. He knew a number of people with the county government, and since his retirement as a maintenance man at the state capital, he had done a variety of jobs for them, such as fixing the huge clock on top of the capitol building. We went to his house until it was time to take the exam.

Then we walked over to the rec center, only a block from his house. He pulled out a door key and let some young people inside to play table tennis. We went to a private area to wait for my appointment. Soon he brought over the lady who'd be giving me my exam. He made introductions and they chatted a bit before it was time for me to fill out the paperwork and complete my interview.

At eighteen, I was mature for my age and had been holding down two jobs as I worked my way through college. I was ahead in my studies, and I worked in the psychology department. I laboriously tabulated test scores in a closet—very boring. My application's references for the civil service job were my psychology and physical education department supervisors who knew me well.

I soon received a response from my application, and I was in for a surprise, to put it mildly. The position offered wasn't for a job with the Social Security Administration in Montgomery; it was for a position in Washington, DC! I couldn't even comprehend what this might lead to. After many long discussions, my parents gave me their blessing to accept the job. I felt like I was in for a great, exciting adventure.

Mother made arrangements for me to stay with Uncle Zed's daughter (my cousin), Mildred Mahan. Milly was a Navy WAVE who lived in Arlington, Virginia, a suburb of Washington, DC. This would work out perfectly! One of my mother's friends planned a bon voyage party, and it was a complete surprise. All my closest friends showed up and brought gifts, wishing me the best of luck. I was very touched by their love and support. It meant so much that they did this for me.

In anticipation of the trip, I got busy packing my wardrobe trunk, which was once Mother's. I hung my clothes on the hangers, found a place for my transistor radio, and packed a few trinkets and other gifts from the bon voyage party into the trunk's drawers.

Daddy took us to Birmingham in his red power company truck on the day I left home. I was going to catch Amtrak's Crescent train from Birmingham to Washington, DC. Thankfully Daddy shipped my trunk to Milly's address in Arlington beforehand.

On the thirty-mile trip to Birmingham, my emotions were all over the place. Mother and I started bawling before we even got to

US Route 31. Racing through my head were anxious thoughts of leaving home, branching out on my own, and living in DC. It was Memorial Day weekend—definitely a time to remember.

CHAPTER 2

Up to the Challenge

The train from Birmingham, AL, to DC was scheduled to depart at 3:05 p.m. on Monday, and I was set to arrive at my destination Tuesday morning. With apprehension and doubt still plaguing my mind, I bravely boarded the train and found my seat. When the train lurched forward, I realized I was beginning my journey. I was on my own, but I was up to the challenge. I could do this!

When we stopped in Atlanta to take on new passengers, I started walking around a bit. I checked my seat location so I'd remember where it was (this was an earlier lesson I'd learned from riding a train to visit my grandmother years before). I wandered into a car where people were sitting in comfortable seats, reading newspapers, chatting, or just looking out the windows, watching the countryside pass by. I settled in for a while and took a seat, hoping to calm my nerves and enjoy the scenery. Many times while growing up, Mother would call us to the dinner table by shouting, "Dinner's ready! Dining car in the rear!" Now I heard that familiar call: "Dining car's open!" and it reminded me of Mother. I missed her already.

I wanted to be responsible and save as much money as possible. I wasn't sure how much I'd need, so I decided not to eat an evening meal in the dining car. Instead, hoping to stay within my budget, I found a vending machine and dropped in a few coins to purchase a snack. I felt like an adult, making adult decisions. So many new experiences on that train trip.

After a long, restless night, I finally stepped off the train in DC's Union Station. I was still wearing the cotton blouse and broomstick skirt I had on when I left Alabama the day before. My Sunday pumps, as opposed to my comfortable saddle oxfords, gave me the confidence of a working girl. The new purse I purchased for the trip contained instructions on where to go, so I held onto it tightly. Even while I still clung to a bit of anxiety, it was soon overshadowed by confidence in my new experience and the thrill of starting an important job. I was ready to report to the address on the telegram I'd received with the job offer. This job was extremely important to me. I'd left my home and come a long way for this. I had to get it right.

Daddy had told me to look for the nearest taxi stand as soon as I got off the train. I was to find a driver and let them know where I needed to go. Montevallo, my hometown, was small—you could walk from one end to the other—and I'd never even seen a taxi before, much less ridden in one. I got off the train and picked the first driver I saw, which caused a huge ruckus. It scared me, but I tried not to let my nervousness show. Once in the taxi and underway, all I could do was stare out the window in amazement. We zipped by the Washington Monument and other famous landmarks I'd only seen in books, and I was mesmerized. To say the vibrant city of Washington, DC, was different from Montevallo was a gross understatement. It was intimidating to think that my cousin Milly was the only person I knew there, but at the same time, my excitement was through the roof.

The taxi driver pulled up to the address I'd given him, and it was a gigantic, official government-looking building. I paid the driver and waited for my change, not knowing anything about tipping. Poor guy. Although he might've guessed my small-town roots from my accent.

I didn't know what to expect as I walked inside the building. A woman was sitting at a desk in the hallway. I showed her my papers, and she directed me into a large room where about a hundred girls had gathered, all waiting to be assigned like me. I saw one of the few chairs left and went to the back of the room to sit to wait. It was hard to ignore my growling stomach and racing heart. I waited and waited, then waited some more. After what seemed like an eternity, a woman entered the room and called out the names for the WAC (Women's Army Corps) assignments. Many young women promptly stood and filed out to go into another room. Then, another list of names was called. This group was being assigned to the Navy WAVES (Women Accepted for Volunteer Emergency Service). They, too, filed out together. Now, oddly, I was the only living soul left in that big, hot room.

The constant tick of the clock on the wall was amplified in that huge, empty space. My anxiety grew with every minute that passed. I felt panic rise from somewhere deep inside and noticed my quick, shallow breaths. The stifling heat of the room pressed in on me, causing my thoughts to run rampant. *Why is my name not being called? Have they forgotten me? Am I in the wrong place?*

After a while, the woman came back in. She walked the long distance across the room, looking at me all the while. I was a little intimidated. I straightened up in my chair, trying to gather my nerves. She spoke in a low voice, as if she didn't want anyone to overhear what she was saying.

"Peggy Mahan Davis?"

"Yes," I replied.

She handed me a large envelope filled with papers, told me to report to another address (quite a distance away), and turned to leave.

I could not wait to get outside.

CHAPTER 3

Keeping Secrets

Finally out of that stuffy government building, I started walking to my new destination. After a short distance, the back of my heels began to burn and blisters started to form. Saddle oxfords seemed a lot more desirable than the Sunday pumps I was wearing.

When I arrived, I stared at the place I'd been sent to with disbelief, thinking surely I made a wrong turn. The building was dilapidated, seemingly abandoned. I wondered if this was even the correct address. Trying to open the heavy wooden doors only scared me more. Putting my full weight into it, I nearly stumbled down the steps into the cramped, dark side entrance of the rickety building.

After my eyes adjusted to the darkness, I saw a uniformed guard immediately stand up. It looked as if I'd startled him awake, and I saw his hand next to the holstered pistol at his side. I tried to contain the frightening wave of panic I felt coming over me. I pulled myself together and hastily showed him my papers. He pointed to a door and told me to go to the secretarial pool. *Did I hear him correctly? What on earth is a secretarial pool?* I'd never heard of secretaries referred to as a *pool* before. Little did I know it was the first of dozens of terms I'd learn on my new job.

I went upstairs where a stern woman looked at my papers and told me to take a typing test. She left the room, giving me an opportunity to check out my surroundings. There were many desks in the room, but only a few were taken. The repetitive tap, tap, tap of typewriter keys was a familiar sound that thankfully calmed my nerves a bit. I easily passed the typing test.

When the woman returned, she handed me yet another set of papers. She said I'd be working for the OSS and instructed me to tell no one about my job. *No one?* This was totally unexpected; now I was really scared!

OSS? What on earth does that mean? If the woman with no smile told me what those letters meant, I never heard it. I was far too nervous. I traveled all this way to work for my country, and I'd just been given the worst assignment ever. This was horrible! Not at all the picture I'd envisioned for my first grown-up job. I could feel heat mounting behind my eyes and knew I was close to tears, but I was determined to hold them off as long as possible.

So far I'd not encountered one person with even a trace of the southern hospitality I was used to. Everyone was so gruff, and nothing but the scenery was what I expected. I was convinced I'd made the biggest mistake of my life, and already I felt like a failure. Descending back down the narrow stairway, I summoned the courage to ask the sleepy guard to call a taxi for me. It was getting late, and I needed to get to the address Milly sent to Mother before anything else could go wrong.

CHAPTER 4

The Oh-So-Secret Agency

Milly's official title was Mildred Mahan, Yeoman 1st Class, and she'd been in the Navy WAVES for two years. She was five years older than me, and we were more like acquaintances than cousins. There she was, the only living soul I knew in DC, yet in truth, I didn't really know her at all. All I knew for sure was that I had to depend on her.

In the taxi on my way to my new home, I continued to stare out the window, numb and exhausted. We crossed over a bridge, and there was the biggest graveyard I'd ever seen, dotted with thousands of white crosses. It was beautiful in its own, sad way.

At the Fort Myer North Gate, about two miles from Washington, DC, the driver made a left turn into a large apartment complex. *Mother would be happy to know I've made it to the address she gave me,* I thought. Milly had been staying temporarily with some married-couple friends but would be moving into an apartment in the four-unit complex across the street now that I was here.

Milly was still at work when I knocked on her friends' door. A woman welcomed me and lent a sympathetic ear as I described the nerve-wracking events of the day. As we talked, I noticed my wardrobe trunk standing against the wall. It triggered thoughts about my clothes hanging in there with my little radio and other trinkets tucked away inside. Just the thought of it caused a swell of nostalgia to sweep through me. This was the trunk that had stood open in my small, upstairs bedroom for several years. It made me homesick.

I could no longer hold back tears, nor did I even want to. Through one sob after another, I blurted out to Milly's friend, "They singled me out because I'm from Alabama! They must think I'm some ignorant southerner!" This was the mid-1940s, and in many ways folks from the Deep South were thought to be backward and uneducated, still rebels at heart. Even movies portrayed southern characters as stupid fools using false accents. *They don't know me; I'm no fool!*

When Milly came in from work, I poured out my heart all over again. I gave her vivid pictures of the emotions and fears I felt when being left alone in that gigantic, stuffy room with a no-nonsense guard and a woman with no smile who made me take a typing test, and a horrible old building, and how I got the bad end of an assignment with the OSS and made a huge mistake coming here, and now I don't have enough money to go back home!

Milly's lips began to curl upward into a smile as I told her about the dreadful assignment with the OSS. Then her smile turned into laughter. She tried to comfort me and calm my raw emotions.

"The OSS is a special elite organization even more protected from the public eye than the Naval Intelligence Office where I work," she said. I was shocked to discover that Milly was working in intelligence. Her smile slowly disappeared as she spoke. "My work is hush-hush, but OSS is a mystery to *everyone* in Washington, DC. OSS stands for the Office of Strategic Services, but we all call it the Oh-So-Secret Agency."

Well, this changed everything! Suddenly I felt special, and all the bad events of the day melted away. This sounded incredibly exciting! I felt a new courage taking hold of me because, ultimately,

I knew I was not a quitter. It was not in my nature to give up. I made the conscious decision right then and there to take Milly at her word and trust my loving parents who put me on that train.

Wiping my tear-streaked face, I determined to give my very best to this new job. I'd been singled out after all! Chosen for top-secret work. Surely this would be an incredible opportunity to make a difference. I was very relieved and very proud that I'd made the right decision. I could uphold my duty to help in the American war effort, even if I couldn't tell anyone about my job. Suddenly all my plans seemed to fall back into place, and I was on solid ground once again.

CHAPTER 5

Top-Secret Typist

I remember the details of it all today—at ninety-nine—as if I were still that same, nervous eighteen-year-old starting a new job in a new city in a new apartment away from home and everything familiar and comfortable to me. That era was life-changing, as wartime often is.

Milly's furniture was already in the new apartment across the street from her married friend and a block from the North Post Gate of Fort Myer in Arlington, VA. The bus stopped there, and I'd be catching it into DC for work every day. We moved in on June 1st, 1944. The apartment was sparsely decorated—if you could call it decorated. There was barely a piece of furniture per room. There was a tiny galley kitchen and no dining room but a kitchen table inside the living room with one chair. There was one threadbare sofa and a sitting chair in the living room. The other kitchen chair was in the bedroom, where Milly and I both shared a double bed.

We weren't very motivated to come home, and each of us found our own way to entertain ourselves.

A telegram was waiting for me in Milly's mailbox. I didn't know how that telegram arrived at our new place. I only knew Mother made all the arrangements with Milly. It made me feel important; I'd never received a telegram before.

The telegram read,

YOUR APPOINTMENT AS CLERK-TYPIST CAF-2 $1440 PER ANNUM, PLUS OVERTIME WITH THIS AGENCY APPROVED CALL MISS BOWEN EXECUTIVE 6100 EXENSION 2638 EARLIEST DATE YOU CAN REPORT FOR DUTY

I called Miss Bowen to let her know the earliest date I could start working. I figured she'd give me further details about where to go and who I'd be meeting. Since I didn't know how to get to my new job, Milly and I rode the bus the next day so I could learn the route to the OSS offices. We crossed over the same bridge I'd crossed the day before. I learned it was the 14th Street Memorial Bridge. We also passed the huge graveyard again, which Milly said was Arlington National Cemetery. The next day I was on my own. With nervous excitement I arrived at 501 26th Street, NW, the main office of the OSS.

I walked to the North Building and reported to Mr. Mayo, a civil service executive in the procurement and supplies department, who graciously welcomed me. He buzzed for Captain Howard J. Preston, who'd been expecting me and would be my immediate boss. They reinforced repeatedly that the work I'd be doing was strictly confidential, top-secret, and I absolutely could not talk to *anyone* about it. They gave me my ID badge and drilled into me that I couldn't let it be seen outside of the office.

Captain Preston took me to the office on the second floor and showed me my desk. There were about eight enlisted men, plus Captain Preston, Captain Tranes, and Major Fisher. The only women were me and Captain Preston's personal secretary.

During my first days I learned about my officemates. Captain Preston's secretary was *not* friendly. She seemed to do very little work, no one talked to her, and she often didn't even show up for work. She didn't lunch with the other girls in the building and was never socially involved with her coworkers. I wasn't accustomed to this attitude and found it distasteful. I was from the South, where people were—and still are—known for their friendliness and hospitality.

Even though he had his own secretary, it wasn't unusual for Captain Preston to stand at my desk to dictate correspondence, which I typed as he spoke. I'd provide him with a draft of his letter, which he'd revise, then hand it to his own secretary later to type a final copy.

Because of my desk's location, everyone spoke to me when they came into the room. One day I got brave and asked Captain Tranes about a tall, young, bearded man wearing a white uniform and walking about the OSS offices. Captain Tranes told me the striking visitor was a former Russian prince who'd been injured during an altercation with a royal family member. Apparently he'd grown the beard to hide a scar that might identify him. I thought Captain Tranes was kidding, but I was oh-so-curious nonetheless.

Recently, however, I came across an online article written by the US National Park Service (NPS) about the OSS, and in their article, they mentioned a fifty-one-year-old former Russian prince, Serge Obolensky, who went through the rigors of two of the OSS's training camps. He also helped write a training manual and schedule for their Operational Groups (OGs), running mock reconnaissance missions to prepare future OSS agents for tactical missions overseas. Now I believe that this was the same former Russian prince wearing an all-white uniform that I saw in the OSS offices in 1944!

CHAPTER 6

Supplies for Our Spies

My official title was *clerk typist*. I kept detailed records of supplies that came and went through procurement and supplies. I stayed busy keeping deliveries in order and routing them to their correct location, which (for me) was always Calcutta (Kolkata), located in India. I had no idea what I was ordering, much less why. Nor did I know where the supplies were headed once they left Calcutta. I ordered supplies with code names, like "Hedy Lamarr," "Aunt Jemima," "Joe Lewis," "Fog Signal," "Joan-Eleanor," "Who Me," "Matchbox," and "101 Project." One day I saw the reference to "101 Project" and blurted out, "I thought I finished my Freshman 101 classes." I was trying to be funny. Sometimes, I was.

Many terms like *Project MO, MU,* and *SI* had no meaning to me. I remember now seeing ink in various colors being ordered by the gallons. I thought the ink was going to someone printing propaganda. Maybe there was a lot of printing going on in Asia? China? I did know what I sent to Calcutta was flown "over the hump" someplace. I finally asked, "What does 'over the hump' mean?" I learned the "hump" was the Himalayan Mountains in Southeast Asia, between China and India, which suggested to me the supplies were going into China. I pictured an OSS agent in the Asian vegetation hiding somewhere, impatiently waiting on the supplies I'd routed his way from my desk in Washington, DC. I didn't ask questions about the supplies, but I was certainly curious.

While working at the OSS, I took art classes at the Corcoran Gallery of Art, which, interestingly, was the first institution in the US created specifically as an art museum. One morning I made mention to Captain Preston that there sure were a lot of plaster statues in that art gallery. He informed me "Aunt Jemima" was a code name for a material something like plaster of paris or flour. He said "Aunt Jemima" was used to make explosives molded to look like statues—as copycats similar to the real ones I'd seen, or rocks, candles, even loaves of bread—and, unbelievably, cow poop! Anything that could be created to deceive. These items were used to blow up bridges or explode when stepped on or thrown against a hard surface. Our secret spies and allies overseas used these tools of the trade to sabotage the enemy.

I realized I was dealing with dangerous wartime supplies. Several times I was sent to the Willard Hotel in downtown DC to deliver a small package. I was told to leave the package at the front desk for the room number I'd been given. When I walked inside that fancy hotel the first time, I was so impressed with the magnificence of the interior. I'd never been inside a hotel before.

Once I was told the package contained nylon stockings, and I might be robbed if anyone knew what I was delivering. I thought that was a joke, but I was never certain. Nylon stockings were off limits, after all, to regular girls like me. The government conserved all nylon during the war to make parachutes, airplane fuel tanks, mosquito netting, hammocks, tents, and more. So American women had to make do with cotton stockings, which snagged and drooped, or else create their own *bottled stockings*. Bottled stockings were painted onto women's shaved legs using an eyeliner pencil or special paint to draw a seam up the center of the backs of their legs to look like real stockings.

CHAPTER 7

On Edge

A major's office was next to where I worked. It wasn't Major Fisher; this was a different one. Usually, when *this* major heard my heels clicking as I passed by, he'd whistle. I'd always whistle back for fun. He'd laugh and sometimes call me in to chat. One day his secretary asked me to go to lunch with her. Later he called me into his office and said, "I heard you went to lunch with my secretary."

"Yes," I said.

"You know, she's a lesbian."

I didn't say anything.

"Do you know what that means?"

Naturally I didn't, but I replied, "She's from Lesbia, I guess."

Oh, he thought that was just hilarious, and I'm sure he told anyone he could about it. Everyone quickly realized I was a straight shooter and a church-going person, and they teased me about being a young, wet-behind-the-ears college student. My southern accent was also a sure-fire source of amusement for everyone.

On another occasion, the secretary of an executive in our department was scheduled to be out for a week. The executive asked

Captain Preston if I could fill in for her. When I walked into his office, the executive looked me up and down and quipped, "That's a nice dress."

"I made it," I proudly replied, not missing a beat. I wasn't comfortable working for this man with wandering eyes but felt committed to cover for his secretary.

During that week he suggested I check out an opportunity for membership with a special group of young girls. The lady interviewing me casually chatted, checked me over, and made it clear what the group was all about. She said I'd enjoy going out to special events with officers as their date, and she tried to make it sound like fun. Without hesitation I let her know I had no interest whatsoever in what she was suggesting. I wasn't too surprised this executive set me up for that meeting; his behavior should've been a clue. I decided before the week was up to avoid him as much as possible in the future.

I never ventured into other sections of the OSS complex. I pretty much stuck to the same routes, taking the shortest paths between buildings, which often meant walking outside. Such was the case with the on-site cafeteria, located behind the complex on the Potomac River.

A fellow in the field photography department took notice of me and my office friends as we made our daily trips for lunch. One day while we were eating, he showed up and introduced himself as part of the photography division of the OSS. We chatted for a while, and he proposed him and I meet for lunch in the cafeteria the next day. He suggested that after lunch we could walk along the Potomac, and he'd shoot some pictures of me. I thought that'd be an unusual and interesting experience. I'd never sat for a photographer before and was flattered by his offer.

The next day we met for lunch, then strolled along the Potomac River as he'd previously suggested. As we walked, he found several scenic spots where he asked me to pose as he shot photos. At one point he asked me to sit on a fallen log and raise my skirt to show more of my legs. I guess he thought I was more naive than I was. I didn't like that one bit. He told me he'd give me some of the pictures. Later, I saw him again in the cafeteria, and he handed over a couple of the pictures he'd taken. He asked where I lived and offered more pictures if I'd go out with him. *A date?* I didn't think that was a good idea. After the log incident he didn't impress me as a safe date, so I never got the rest of the photographs.

Another time a sailor boy, the son of an office acquaintance, invited me for a moonlight canoe ride on the Potomac. My only previous canoe ride was with the Senior Girl Scouts in Montevallo, where I'd learned to row and earned my water sports badge. Once again, I was excited about the prospect but ended up disappointed. I wasn't impressed at all. In fact, it seemed I knew more about canoeing than he did. Although I enjoyed the moonlit view, I didn't enjoy being with that young man and didn't see him again.

One day I and some other girls working in the OSS offices were asked to volunteer to attend a social event at the Congressional Country Club in Bethesda, Maryland. It was a generous invitation, and there was a busload of us. My girlfriend and I wondered what to expect. Dancing? Barbeque? I'm glad my fifteen-year-old brother, Willard, and I had taught ourselves the jitterbug to good old swing music. When we arrived at the Country Club, a large group of OSS military men greeted our bus. The event had been well planned—a party atmosphere in a magnificent building, as it should be. All the men were probably following orders to be on good behavior. One of my dance partners let it slip that the Club's nickname was "Malice in Wonderland," though. I've since learned it was called that because it's where OSS trainees learned the dirty tricks of warfare.

It was a hot summer evening, and I did my share of jitterbug dancing to loud swing and jukebox music. No slow dancing there—lots of excited merriment best described the mood. That was the first time I'd ever danced with someone other than my younger brother.

During the evening, no questions were asked, and there was no shop talk about who the men were or why there were one hundred OSS men at the beautiful Congressional Country Club.

I heard *active training* mentioned a few times, but I had no clue. We were a bunch of sweaty and exhausted girls about to board the bus at the end of the evening, and the guys followed us out to bid farewells. I wondered how this beautiful facility (a golf course) was being secretly used by the OSS. It was a mystery, but I thought I had an idea of what was going on.

One day when we were headed to the cafeteria, one of my lunch buddies pointed to a window across the way and said, "That's Wild Bill's office." I didn't know who "Wild Bill" was but figured that's where the big boss worked. Later I'd learn he was William J. Donovan, Founder and Director of the Office of Strategic Services—a legend in the DC area. In Washington, DC, politicians and influential society members swam in many of the same circles. President Roosevelt referred to Wild Bill as his "secret-idea" man. But Navy Intelligence considered him a rogue—he didn't like to follow the rules, preferring unconventional ways of getting things done. Now "Wild Bill" Donovan is remembered as the "Father of American Intelligence."

CHAPTER 8

Many More "Firsts"

Outside of work at the OSS, much of my life in Arlington and DC was probably typical of someone my age seeing an unfamiliar world for the first time. There were so many big city *firsts* for a young, rural girl to explore. The first weekend I was in Arlington I found a church within walking distance of my and Milly's apartment. I placed my membership and began attending regularly. It was comforting to know I had a church family close by. How happy I was to meet a lovely lady who'd graduated from Montevallo College. She and her husband invited me to Sunday dinner in their home several times.

I adjusted and felt more secure as I began to find my place in that city. A youth group at church had regular socials, and its minister worked at the White House. His wife said, "He's a *housekeeping engineer*." I didn't ask about that funny remark as others laughed. One of the group activities was bowling, which was foreign to me. Coming from a small-town culture, Mother wouldn't allow us to go bowling. She said bowling alleys weren't a place for children or young girls; it was a men's hangout place for smoking and playing pool. That was the first time I ever bowled—and I quite liked it.

With my bus pass, I soon became familiar with the area and could hardly wait to visit all the monuments and museums. A few times on Sunday afternoons, I'd enjoy a string quartet concert at the National Gallery of Art and often did repeat tours of the Smithsonian. I toured the Capitol, the White House, and Ford's Theatre where President Lincoln was assassinated. I enjoyed the Library of Congress and the Jefferson Memorial too. It was a beautiful spring in DC, especially with the cherry blossoms in full bloom. Roaming around DC was another *first*, and it was a delight.

Usually I was alone as I explored the city, and my confidence was growing. But on one of my bus rides, I had a memorable scare. I sat on the aisle seat with a young colored girl about my age who was reading. As she looked up I greeted her and asked what her book was about. She said, "Sociology 101." I replied, "Been there. Just finished my 101 classes," and we talked a little. We crossed the river from DC into Virginia, and I soon learned that Blacks could sit anywhere they wanted in our nation's capital, but not in Virginia.

The huge, overweight bus driver strode back to our seat. Leaning over me but talking directly to her, he spat out, "Get up and go to the back of the bus!" I was startled. She stood to obey him, and I moved into the aisle to let her out. She began to walk toward the back. I followed her. The bus driver seemed confused. He stood there and stared at us, then went back to his driver's seat, but I kept seeing him checking us in his rearview mirror. My seatmate and I were too afraid to speak again. Thank goodness we were nearly to Fort Myer, where I gladly got off that bus and left its hostile driver behind. It was a very awkward situation.

Two nice sergeants in my office, Jack and Peanut, became my lunchtime friends right away. They invited me to go with them to Glen Echo Park. A *park* they said, so I anticipated a walk in the park. I had no clue it was a famous amusement park, and it was another exciting first for me. My only experience prior had been the traveling carnival on a corner in Montevallo, which only had a Ferris wheel and a merry-go-round.

On another occasion, a group of office guys invited me to go with them to their favorite restaurant for a steak dinner. It was something they did regularly on Friday nights, and, coincidentally, it was in Fort Myer, near my apartment and the PX (a discount retail store for military personnel and their families). They were kind to invite me to tag along. Much to their amusement, they discovered I'd never ordered a steak before. I knew nothing about rare, medium, medium-well, or well-done choices. I'd eaten country fried steak but not the kind of steak the servicemen were ordering. I thoroughly enjoyed my steak, though, and they enjoyed teasing their new southern belle friend who didn't even know the difference between rare and well-done.

I had a membership at the YWCA and swam there regularly. The Y was on 17th and K Streets. Often during hot, summer days, I walked to the Y and enjoyed a swim. I even had my first massage one evening after swimming. *Oh boy, I'm living the good life!*, I thought to myself.

I asked Milly to meet me at the Y for a swim one evening, and she reminded me she didn't know how to swim. She and several of her WAVE friends needed to learn to swim so they could be eligible for their next Navy promotions. Having already earned my Red Cross instructor certification, I mentioned to the administrator at the Y that I'd be happy to teach a swimming class, telling her about Milly and her friends. The administrator was delighted to have me, especially as I'd already gathered enough adults together to fill a beginner swimming class. She checked my Alabama references and offered me the opportunity. Another first: teaching a swimming class.

Milly often met me at a drugstore near my office where we'd have a snack before going to the pool. One day, we were eating and chatting in a booth, and the waitress came over to ask if I might be Peggy Davis from Alabama. Pointing to four smiling Annapolis cadets in another booth, she said, "One of those guys knows you." I confirmed I was Peggy Davis, and two of the Navy cadets joined us in our booth. The boy who'd recognized me was actually a distant cousin, Henry Mahan. The other young cadet sat across from me with expressive eyes and introduced himself as Jimmy Carter from Plains, Georgia. Trying to be funny, I responded, "I thought the plains were in the West, not Georgia." I totally forgot about this little meeting until many years later when I saw pictures of our nation's thirty-ninth president in his Annapolis uniform. Seeing the uniform, I looked closer and realized that man was my cousin's friend whom I'd met in Washington, DC, in 1945. Jimmy!

I was known in our housing subdivision as a good, qualified babysitter, and I was happy to help the military couples for extra money. One lady had a sewing machine I could use, and I was so happy about that. Soon I had the opportunity to ride into work with a neighbor, along with a few other courteous men. I was able to babysit for one of them, and that turned out to be my good fortune. Now I could ride to work with them instead of catching the bus. I loved it!

Milly wanted us to plan a party. She knew I worked in an office full of men, so she asked me to invite some of them, saying she'd invite her WAVE friends too. I was embarrassed to be issuing invitations to friends who were just office acquaintances. It didn't seem appropriate, but I didn't want to disappoint Milly. With hesitancy, I invited Peanut and Jack. It was fun discovering Peanut liked to jitterbug. We had a good time that evening. It was my first grown-up house party. I was surprised the downstairs neighbors didn't complain, though, with the radio blasting and their ceiling shaking from all the jumping around.

The party atmosphere was exciting, but I was a bit embarrassed. I'd only been familiar with teen parties at our Girl Scout house, or in someone's home in Montevallo. This was a very different kind of party, complete with brash, wartime adult conversation and beer. I certainly was not comfortable with that situation. Later I learned that Jack must've been engaged at the time because I soon got invited to his wedding. Peanut and I remained friends and had a few dates before he left for an overseas assignment.

November 5th, 1944: my birthday. I was turning nineteen years old and was still with the OSS. When I left Alabama, I'd thought the job would only be for the summer, but I was there to do my duty, and the job wasn't finished. We hadn't won the war yet.

Milly planned a birthday getaway for me, a hike in the beautiful Harpers Ferry Historical National Park in West Virginia. This was just my kind of party and my first time out of the busy city. We took a train ride for a tour of this Civil War-era park. I felt like we were in another world while we enjoyed nature in West Virginia. It was a beautiful countryside.

Later, as the new year rolled around, I attended my coworker Jack's wedding in Saint John's Episcopal Church, across from Lafayette Park near the White House. This was the first Catholic church and formal wedding I'd ever been to. When I was in my young teens, I was asked to sing at a small wedding in Montevallo, but being at a formal wedding in a famous church in Washington, DC, was awe-inspiring. The setting, the formality, the music, the kneeling bench—I'd never seen anything like it.

Major Fisher, whose desk was right behind mine, was from Knoxville, Tennessee. He was the only other southerner in our large office, and we often had chats about various things. Soon after I met him, I learned he was a pianist. I mentioned to him I'd attended a piano concert at college the previous year. Come to find out, the pianist was his friend Eugene List, and that launched our office friendship. Major Fisher and his wife invited me to a symphony concert at an amphitheater-type venue on the Potomac River, to which I wore the dress I'd made while babysitting. That musical experience was certainly another thrilling addition to my brightly colored life of divergent experiences in Washington, DC.

Milly and I had several visitors. One weekend, her brother in the Merchant Marines and a friend of his were in town. They took Milly and me to a well-known, local nightclub. This was another first for me. They ordered me a sloe gin fizz and told me it was just a flavored soda—no alcohol. It tasted so good, I ordered another. I didn't know if I was tipsy or not, but I sure was laughing a lot! They had fun playing this trick on me.

Another time, the two oldest of my six brothers, John and Willard, also came to visit me. They both had jobs. They were teenagers, and they'd saved their money for the big trip. We visited Mount Vernon, the local monuments, and other tourist points of interest. I took them to a movie where we were ushered to the first row. I complained to the usher, but he explained we could move when seats were available. I had no idea a live stage show was about to begin.

Three performers on roller skates appeared on stage and began their routine. After a while, the leader of the group rolled to the edge of the stage and called for a volunteer from the audience to come onstage. He looked down at me, extending his hand, and said, "How about you, young lady?" I was shocked and embarrassed and resisted, but my brothers began pushing me toward the stage. The group leader pulled me up onto the stage and, holding onto my hands, began to twirl me around and around on his skates while I couldn't help but scream. He spun me so fast my shoes flew off. When he stopped, I was dizzy, unsteady, and couldn't stop holding onto him for balance. He loved it. He made quick remarks like, "She likes me," and, "Where are her shoes?" Comments that made the audience laugh. The biggest laughs came after he asked the audience if there were any holes in my socks. My brothers thoroughly enjoyed all this commotion, but I was mortified!

CHAPTER 9

Deep. Loss.

On April 12th, 1945, around 5:00 p.m., I left work and stopped at the neighborhood drugstore for a bite to eat before going to the Corcoran Gallery of Art for my painting class. A manager came out from a mezzanine office, shouting, "President Roosevelt's dead!" I ran to the Corcoran, located on 17th Street across from the White House. A convertible was parked nearby with a gathering crowd listening to a radio news report, and I watched a man walk down the edge of the White House roof to lower the American flag. A limousine whizzed by. I'd learn later it was bringing Eleanor Roosevelt home from a speaking engagement.

I stood in shock, not believing what was happening. I walked around the White House to Lafayette Park and sat on a bench facing the White House to calm my nerves and think about what had occurred and what could happen next. *What does the future hold for our country?* I sat there a long time as a crowd began to gather in the park and official limousines started entering the White House gates. As it got dark, people gathered holding candles.

I kept thinking how the year was just beginning for our President Roosevelt. He'd been sworn in for his fourth consecutive term of office on January 20th, 1945. In early February, he'd joined Great Britain's prime minister, Winston Churchill, and the Soviet Union's dictator, Josef Stalin, at the Yalta Conference, held in Crimea.

President Franklin D. Roosevelt passed away at his summer home in Warm Springs, Georgia. For years, residents there welcomed him and gave him privacy in their small town. Newspapers wrote about his get-away-from-DC trips to The Little White House in Warm Springs. The eighty-eight-degree hot springs water was therapeutic for his polio. It was his place of respite.

At the time of his death, he was sitting in his chair, posing for a portrait in the company of his cousins and special friend Lucy Mercer Rutherford when he collapsed at 1:15 p.m. At 5:47 p.m., the White House's press secretary sent out a statement saying the president had died of a cerebral hemorrhage. Eleanor had gotten a call earlier saying he had fainted. She wrote later in her memoir, "That ride to the White House was one of dread."

By the following morning, radio stations reported a funeral train had left Warm Springs the night before, bringing Roosevelt's flag-draped coffin to Washington, DC. News reports described the farewell of loyal Warm Springs citizens: hundreds of them lined the railroad tracks in respect as their beloved townsman's body left them. Thousands of people later lined the tracks all the way to Washington, DC, to say goodbye to America's popular thirty-second president.

The train came into Union Station the morning of April 13th, where another funeral procession formed along the streets to the White House. I took the bus from the apartment into the city for this event. After the White House funeral on April 14th, 1945, Roosevelt was transported by train from Washington, DC to his place of birth in Hyde Park, New York. On April 15th, he was buried, per his wish, in the rose garden of his Springwood estate.

Roosevelt had been president since I was in the second grade. We'd read about him in our *Weekly Reader* newspaper as elementary school kids. He had contracted polio in August 1921. The March of

Dimes campaigns were originally established for polio research, not birth defects. When I went to work in DC, I knew he had polio, but the public never knew the full extent of his crippling condition. I learned a wheelchair ramp existed at the Tomb of the Unknown Soldier at Fort Myer, across the street from where Milly and I lived. I was surprised to find out that ramp was there for the president.

CHAPTER 10

The End of the War of All Wars

While working for America's Office of Strategic Services, World War II officially ended in Europe on May 8th, 1945. Known as VE (Victory in Europe) Day, this day celebrated the formal acceptance by the allies of Germany's unconditional surrender of its armed forces, marking the end of WWII in Europe. On June 10th, 1945, General Dwight David Eisenhower, in celebration of VE Day, came to Washington, DC, after his visit in New York City. We were all encouraged to walk to the Lincoln Memorial to welcome him. I stood alone, right there on the curb, shouting and waving to him in his convertible with his wife, Mamie, his son, John, and young grandson, David.

One of many soldiers standing at attention and lining the curb was positioned right in front of me. He passed out, hitting the street and crushing his glasses, just as the general passed by. What a shock! I instinctively reached down to help him up, but the guard next to him whispered, "Leave him alone, he'll be OK." I was amazed when the injured soldier stood right back up to attention, bloody face and all. I offered him my handkerchief as I handed him his crushed eyeglasses. Nobody else responded to his collapse. I walked back to the office as the crowd dispersed, thinking I should've done more to help him.

In August, while I was teaching swimming at the YWCA, the Y administrator came out on the balcony above the pool and shouted, "The war is over! They signed the papers!" August 14th, 1945, is the day on which Imperial Japan unconditionally surrendered, bringing the war with Japan to an end. Victory in Japan, VJ Day! This meant World War II was finally over! Both Germany and Japan had been defeated. Of course, we were all *more* than excited. It was the news we'd been waiting for! There was lots of shouting and splashing to get out of the pool.

Milly and her WAVE friends invited me to celebrate with them, but I knew I didn't fit in their circle. I left the Y alone, walking out onto the street already covered with festive, young government workers and servicemen. I was startled by the blasting sounds of people shouting, screaming, and singing. Added to the noise were car, truck, and city bus horns blown in repeated unison. Huge throngs of people were everywhere. The sidewalks and streets were totally covered with revelers. *Maybe I should've been a tag-along with Milly and her friends after all.*

Right away I saw men kissing young ladies they met in this exploding party atmosphere. A sailor about my age approached me with a sly grin on his face as he playfully gave me a big, strong hug and kiss. Wow! *What should I do? Think fast. I need protection.* He seemed to be alone as well. I considered this sailor my assurance for a safe walk down to the Pennsylvania Avenue bus station for my ride home. I held his hand tightly to calm my panic reaction to that whole uncontrolled mob. I needed to keep him with me for a while, for certain.

We couldn't move because there were far too many people. We ventured into the crowded street and hopped on the bumper of an expensive-looking, white convertible full of celebrating strangers. We shouted, sang, and waved our arms as the uniformed officer moved his fancy car along at a crawling pace, not really moving in a way of making progress. Eventually we got back onto the sidewalk for me to make an urgent effort to get to the bus station while the buses were still on schedule. I felt secure in this bedlam with my new escort who got me safely to the station. After another friendly farewell kiss, we exchanged addresses. We corresponded with each other a few times after I returned to college. He went back to Stanford, CT, his home state, while I returned to Montevallo.

Victory celebrations were over. For me, work had lost its urgency. My contribution to WWII was complete. I now needed to re-focus my energies on my own life and future. It was August 1945. The time was right for me to return to college. Yes, time to go back home to Alabama. The fall semester would be starting soon. I planned to return to the simple rhythm of the life I'd had before I ran off to Washington, DC, to do my duty for my country.

I later learned that all the OSS records were classified and would be declassified after fifty years. There were many questions in my mind: *Why were the supplies flown "over the hump" to be dropped who knows where?* I wondered if I'd ever understand why I'd been keeping records of supplies going to Calcutta, India. *The Burma Road? China? Guerrilla Warfare? Civil Wars? Bridges destroyed? Black propaganda?* So many questionable phrases. And so, I've kept those memories locked away in my mind for five decades after the end of the war of all wars.

CHAPTER 11

Wrapping Up

A trip to New York City was still on my bucket list before returning home to Alabama. In late August 1945, my friend from Montevallo, Pat Weems, came for a visit, and Captain Tranes enthusiastically planned our whole weekend of sightseeing. Captain Tranes lived in New York and always returned home on the weekends to be with his family. He had often encouraged me to visit New York City, so now we had plans.

Our personal New York tour package included a visit to Radio City Music Hall, where we sat in on a broadcast. We visited Chinatown and saw the Broadway play *Life with Father* at the Empire Theatre. We took a boat trip up the Hudson River and saw the Statue of Liberty. A young couple on the Hudson River tour tried to play matchmaker by introducing us to a couple of servicemen on that same boat. The couple suggested we continue our tour with the boys, which did make the tour more special. Servicemen were deeply appreciated and respected as heroes and friends to everyone in that wartime culture.

I felt so lucky to experience a New York City ticker-tape parade during our girls trip! General Charles de Gaulle from France was being welcomed to the City by a cheering crowd. We'd been unaware of any scheduled appearance, but there he was with Mayor Fiorello La Guardia. I'd seen ticker-tape parades in movies and news reports, but the real New York scene was spectacular! I was so impressed with de Gaulle and his entourage, waving to the public on their way to City Hall for a ceremonial welcome. As the parade passed by, a garbage truck followed close behind, sweeping the streets to remove the ticker tape scattered about.

That New York City trip was my last big adventure in 1945. On Friday, August 24th, I wrote a letter to my family letting them know my plans for leaving my job and returning to Alabama. Pat was to leave New York on Wednesday, August 29th, taking my packed trunk with her. I'd return to Montevallo the next week and was hoping my sister, Una Faye, would register me at Alabama College for the upcoming fall semester. Once home, I'd pick out my classes.

My initial plan for a summer job in Alabama had turned into a year-and-a-half of work with the OSS in Washington, DC. I had matured so much during that time. I'd met a whole new group of friends, seen the big city with its wonders, and experienced the more seedy side of life as well. I'd learned that southern politeness is often perceived as flirtation by those not accustomed to it. I experienced so many *first evers*, all in the beautiful backdrop of our nation's capital. It was a very, very special time in my life.

There were oh-so-many new things for me to experience as a young adult:

- First time eating in a fast-food restaurant
- First time riding a city bus
- First time buying a winter coat (as opposed to wearing hand-me-downs)
- First time wearing wedge-heeled, summer sandals

- First time drinking coffee
- First time wearing hose

Not only did I do my duty for our country, but I also grew into a woman while doing so.

CHAPTER 12

Home Again

The victory celebrations were over. It was time to return home and get back to college. I wanted to bury anything I'd learned about the OSS deep in my subconscious mind. Before leaving, I was reminded again and again not to talk about my work. Seeing as how I really didn't know anything specific about my job, I never talked about it anyway. I wondered if I'd ever know the answers to my unvoiced questions. All I knew was I did whatever was asked of me for our country. Now, as I think back on everything, I'm proud of myself for having had a small, but necessary, part to play during World War II.

When I returned home, I got right back into the rhythm of life. School, again! Both the physical education and psychology instructors called me, asking if I could work for them. They told me they'd been contacted by "government people" in Washington when I'd first applied in Montgomery for a civil service job. They'd both given me good recommendations and were curious about the "important" work I'd done in DC. They kept asking questions, trying to pry information from me, but it gave me great satisfaction to say I couldn't talk to anyone about it. Needless to say, it made me feel important.

As I returned to college, the feeling of anxiety started creeping back in. I'd loved the adventures working for the OSS and all the various social activities. Now I was back at school—a *nobody*, it seemed. However, that was about to change.

Although my college major was art, I hadn't forgotten my dream of being part of the world of fashion. After meeting with Miss Josephine Eddy in the home economics department, I decided to minor in retail merchandising. Miss Eddy became my advisor and mentor, and we planned out my academic year. Some of my classes included retail home economics, history of clothing, textiles, and sewing.

Miss Eddy suggested the first class I needed was Sewing 101. I showed her the coat I was wearing and told her I'd made it and that I'd been making some of my own clothes since I was eleven. She examined the herringbone twill coat (with a rayon lining) and immediately said, "You certainly don't need Sewing 101." Instead, she scheduled me for an upper-level sewing class, which I called the *draping* class, where we designed clothes. In this class we were to re-fit a dress form to match our own measurements. A dress form is the torso form of a woman, usually made of cloth or wire, mounted on a stand. We created several outfits by draping, pinning, cutting, and sewing. I enjoyed the challenge of not having to follow a pattern. I can be very creative, and I found the class fun, rewarding, and challenging.

Avondale Mills in Sylacauga, AL, was making a new type of cotton fabric called chambray. The mill was well-known for making bed ticking and denim but recently had begun making this beautiful colorful-striped fabric for ladies and children's wardrobes. Avondale was also making a thick-corded fabric for men's suits. They wanted to promote the sale of these new fabrics in well-known department stores. At this time, it was still commonplace for women to make clothes for their children and themselves. Avondale Mills donated these fabrics to several Alabama colleges' home economics departments, and our draping class had the opportunity to use that gifted cloth. I couldn't wait to get my hands on it and eagerly got busy making two outfits.

At the end of the draping class, we had a professional-type fashion show in the college auditorium. Several Avondale Mills officials attended the big affair. I proudly modeled the formal, off one shoulder, blue-striped evening gown I'd created from the dress material. I also showed them a dressy suit I'd made for myself from the corded fabric. I even made a matching hat to add drama to my business-type feminine suit. It was a big hit!

Miss Eddy had chosen each of the classes in my curriculum to prepare me for a real job. The class in retail economics presented an opportunity for me to be an intern in Loveman's Department Store in Birmingham, Alabama's, biggest and busiest city, then and now. I was involved in sales training, store decoration, and comparison shopping where I visited specialty shops and fabric stores. My class in history of dress was intriguing. It gave me insight into how fashions evolve and relate to the current culture. I recognized new dress styles after WWII were becoming more feminine, and I was happy to see that happening.

Since I lived at home and wasn't part of any college social groups, I tried to be more involved in extracurricular activities, including the glee club, college orchestra, religious student council, and various drama groups. I also got involved, again, in the creative productions of College Night, the annual two-day homecoming event held each February. It was the highlight of the year for the college and the local community.

College Night was the culmination of the college's fine arts activities. Students were divided into two teams, gold and purple (the school's colors). The teams competed in theatrical performances planned and created by students. Each team wrote and produced a play (with stunts) and two songs—one rousing, the other slow. These productions were the main event, held both nights of homecoming. I was on the art committee for the gold team and helped with all the art-related planning, including building and painting the scenery. I was also responsible for writing the lyrics and musical score to the slow song. The evening before the opening College Night, alumni, students of all ages, and townsfolk were invited to the dress rehearsal where they'd cheer loudly for their team. At the end of the event, the judges would decide the winners. I liked being needed and recognized by my peers, and my involvement in College Night boosted my morale and confidence tremendously.

For students who didn't live on campus, the college provided two rooms for their convenience in the lower level of the main dormitory. There was a large room with two cots, a smaller area with a shower and toilet, and another room for studying, with a long table and straight-backed chairs. It was a place to spend time between classes and work on assignments while on campus. The rooms were rather dreary and unimpressive. I sometimes brought a bag lunch and ate in the study room, but most of the time I'd go home for lunch. I liked Mother's good, hot meals, and she liked that I'd hang the laundry on the clothesline afterwards.

I preferred studying in the library and kept my grades up enough to be on the Dean's List. With a heavy load of classes, a full work schedule, and work at home, there wasn't much free time. I had a job at the pool and managed to make a little extra spending money that way.

The year moved along quickly now that the war was over. Families were reunited, and there was a general feeling of optimism in the air. Men returned home from their assignments, and it seemed they were suddenly everywhere. We even had three boys enrolled in our women's college, much to the girls' delight. It was wonderful to see things getting back to normal, and everyone was eager to get on with life, boosted by a new enthusiasm.

CHAPTER 13

Changes Ahead

Miss Eddy, my home economics instructor, gave our class a project. We were to write a term paper pertaining to something we'd learned in class, but we could choose our own topic. She had previously shown me an article in *Fortune* magazine about Avondale Mills, and I decided to use that information for my paper. The article highlighted the textile industry in the South and headlined Avondale Mills. Imagine it—Avondale Mills in *Fortune* magazine!

Miss Eddy and Mrs. Dawn Kennedy (head of the art department) planned a combined class field trip to the mill. We were given a tour of the various departments there and were briefed on the process of fabric production. We were introduced to officials and staff as we went along. Luckily for me, our tour guide was Buddy Woods, whom I knew as the older brother of my friend, Frances Woods. I thought Buddy was rather handsome. I felt as if he was directing the tour exclusively for me. I wonder now if it was as obvious to everyone else that day as it was to me.

One day, as I was walking home from the library, I noticed Buddy was visiting the Lyman house right across the street. I thought he might want to know about the article in *Fortune*. At least I hoped he did. The Lyman house was a neighborhood hangout, and nobody knocked. I walked right in, and there was Buddy. I told him about the article, and we chatted a bit. He did seem interested, and as I left, he followed me out the door and headed to the library to read it for himself.

During my senior year, my friend Tootsie wanted to go to the *big* (college) prom. She wanted me to go with her, and she devised a plan. She'd invite Hal, a friend who was *almost taken* because he was *almost engaged,* and she suggested I invite Buddy. That sounded like a good idea to me! The next time I saw Buddy's car at the Lyman house, it took everything I had to summon up the courage I needed. I told him about Tootsie's plan and asked if he'd like to go with us as my escort. I had the sneaky suspicion that Hal might've told him about the plan beforehand. I was now twenty-two and halfway expected Buddy to decline; he was a "man of the world" and older than I was and might find the prom juvenile or boring. However, he readily accepted my invitation, and Hal accepted Tootsie's. I really didn't expect Buddy to accept and was unprepared. I didn't have anything appropriate to wear but soon managed to borrow a friend's formal dress and long, black gloves.

On the night of the prom, the big gym was nicely decorated for the occasion, and the turnout was good. I'd made sure my dance card was nearly full so Buddy wouldn't feel like he was stuck with me all night. However, he pulled me to a corner of the gym and tried to shy away from the big crowd. He purposely ignored the dance card all evening. "Canary" Anderson, a pretty friend in my art class with long, blonde hair, had roped her brother into escorting her. She made a special effort to find us so she could dance with my date. My only dance partners that night were Buddy and Canary's silly brother. I got the distinct impression that Canary was as interested in Buddy as I was.

I'd already gotten permission to go to Birmingham after the prom for a midnight breakfast. The four of us left the prom a little early, feeling very excited to be going to the city for a midnight breakfast. It seemed very adult-like. It was nice, but the city didn't seem like such a big deal after visiting DC and NYC.

Buddy asked Hal to drive home, which of course meant Buddy and I sat in the back seat. Hal stopped at Mudd's Lake (just outside of Montevallo) for us to look at the moon over the lake. I was very shocked when this nice, shy brother of my friend kissed me before we even got out of the car. Wow! I couldn't believe it! We got out and joined Tootsie and Hal. We stayed for a while, looking at the lake, talking and laughing before we headed home. It was heady stuff for me!

Once home, I realized I was missing one of the long, black gloves I'd borrowed. Oh, for goodness' sake! I had a hard time sleeping from all the excitement. Then I had to call and tell Buddy about my missing glove. I told him I thought it must be in the car or beside the road where we'd parked at the lake. He drove back out there, found the glove, and gallantly brought it back to me. It was awkward and embarrassing, and I told my curious little brothers I'd left the glove in the car. After that prom weekend, Buddy returned to work at Avondale Mills, and I started to think of him more often.

CHAPTER 14

Fortune Smiled On Me

A bit later in the year, Miss Eddy took me to Avondale Mills to interview for a position in their design department. On that visit, I met Ann Watson and Frances Weaver, who had just been hired. They'd recently completed their master's degrees from the University of Alabama, and each had made garments from the new fabrics donated to their school by Avondale. I thought it was surely a sign of good luck to meet those girls. Now I knew, at the very least, that Avondale would hire girls my age.

At the time, I had no assurance of landing a job at the mill, but Miss Eddy was confident and urged me on. It seemed she wanted me to have the job as much as I wanted it, and unbeknownst to me, she'd had a plan all along. She evidently knew the mill was looking to hire girls from Alabama colleges, and the donation of fabrics was part of that plan. Miss Eddy wanted to be sure I had an edge over applicants from other schools. This was a new undertaking for the company, recruiting from colleges. Avondale Mills wanted the students to create and model outfits for showing and promoting their new merchandise. I enjoyed the home economics classes and guidance that eventful year. However, at the time, I didn't realize she was setting the stage for me. Avondale informed us they'd be in touch once a decision was made. I settled in for the wait.

Another unexpected thing happened, and it came from the art department. Mrs. Kennedy wanted me to interview for a job at the Toledo Museum of Art in Toledo, Ohio. I was still awaiting news from the mill, where Miss Eddy was certain they'd choose me, and I totally embraced her enthusiasm. It felt good, and I felt good about myself. I was finding confidence that I didn't have before. I felt appreciated, and I had options!

I told Mrs. Kennedy I wasn't interested in the Toledo job, but she insisted it would be good for me to represent our "little college," and they would pay my expenses. So I traveled to Toledo to check out the museum as a favor to her and to see if it held any potential at all for my future. The museum curator and his secretary-wife were very gracious as they greeted me and gave me a tour of the museum.

That evening, I was invited to their home for a lovely dinner. As we dined, they described their hopes to establish a new, more innovative direction for the museum. They wanted someone to work with them to set up an enrichment program of art classes for housewives and children. Classes would include art appreciation, art history, painting, and crafts, as well as other art-related subjects.

I was never deeply interested, but I soon realized I wasn't qualified either. As we were served a beautiful dessert, they told me the job was mine if I'd accept the offer. I graciously thanked them and truthfully explained my concerns, also mentioning that I was anxiously waiting to hear back from a previous interview in Alabama. I was a bit embarrassed, knowing before coming that my heart wasn't in it. I'd done what Mrs. Kennedy asked of me, and now I could head back home.

It was early June, and graduation was looming. Miss Eddy informed me that I'd been offered the job at Avondale Mills. They'd called her with the good news instead of me, but it didn't even matter. This was incredible! I was so relieved and absolutely on cloud nine. I had a sneaking suspicion that Buddy may've known about my good news before I did. I hadn't seen Buddy since the prom in May, but he was still working at the mill, and we'd been corresponding back and forth. It made checking the mail so much more exciting.

Knowing I had this glamorous job waiting for me when I graduated was so very far above my expectations. I can't overstate to you now just how happy I was. My prayers had been answered. I felt noticed and accepted in the business world. I was on my way. How good could life be?

Spring of 1947 had come and gone quickly, with rewarding accomplishments in college and two job offers. I was on a roll. It was already May, time for our traditional commencement exercise.

Wait! Just a minute!

Then came the unbelievable state of affairs. I was informed I had enough college credits to graduate but not enough residential hours. I couldn't believe my ears! It was just ridiculous. I'd been a part of that college for fifteen years of my education. I didn't understand. This was downright awful. What a turn of events.

Even though I needed to complete those hours before officially graduating, thankfully I was allowed to go through the cap and gown ceremony that spring and receive my diploma. However, I had to stay registered another semester. This meant my great dream job was put on hold. For goodness' sake! My heart wasn't in school anymore. I took a college tennis class and continued to teach children to swim at the pool at the Y for spending money. What joy and relief when I finally finished those residential hours. Now I had my bachelor of arts degree and was eager to become a working girl in that new post-war era.

World, here I come again!

CHAPTER 15

My Dream Job

When I was in the sixth grade, our teacher decided the class would have a store. We brought in empty food cans and other items you'd typically find in a general store. A few of my friends and I decided to have our own stores. One setup was the bank, where my friend Pat Weems was the banker. Another friend was the proprietor of the general store. In my dress shop, I designed fashionable clothing on paper that we passed around as we "wore" them on special occasions. At the time, it never occurred to me that someday I'd actually design and create women's clothing. Now I was launching a new, exciting adventure doing just that.

I was offered a job in the design department at Avondale Mills in Sylacauga, AL, which was different from the jobs most of my peers had. Several of my lifelong friends became teachers after college, but both Pat Weems and I had our sixth-grade dream jobs. She'd always wanted to be a statistician, though she couldn't really even pronounce the word. She began her career as an accountant, and I began mine as a dress designer. Since the war was over and the men were back, opportunities for girls in the job market were now limited. I realized how lucky I was and felt so thankful I had that opportunity.

Sales departments wanted to see new fashions created using new fabrics, and the design department of Avondale Mills needed to see the big picture of how they fit into their marketing strategy. The department was responsible for designing and creating garments for us and others to model. They wanted us to wear our creations all the time, as we were their walking advertisements.

Avondale Mills' president, Hugh Comer, wanted us to select young women from the mill to wear the new clothing lines around in public. He thought it'd be a good public relations move. We looked for female employees who might fill this need and selected several young, attractive girls to walk the runway.

During a promotional trip to the Maid of Cotton pageant in Memphis, TN, I met a lady from a New York modeling agency who was judging the pageant. I asked her for some modeling tips and techniques. She showed me how to walk, move, and feature the fashions on the runway in the best way. After the visit, I showed the mill models what I'd learned so they'd feel more comfortable.

Our garments would be featured in fashion shows promoting the mill's new fabrics. This was the beginning of Avondale Mills' effort to branch out into making textiles and merchandise other than bed ticking and denim. It was their new branding venture. The first fall I worked at Avondale, Ann, Frances, and I were sent on trips to the mill's various sales departments located throughout the country. What a busy, fun time, and it was an enormous learning experience for us as well.

The design department's first big assignment was a visit to the New York City sales department, which was the business headquarters for Avondale Mills. We were there to meet the staff and learn about the business. We were introduced to a very friendly lady who would be our host and guide. She took us on a fashion tour where we visited major dress pattern companies—Simplicity,

McCall's, Vogue, and Butterick. Our tour also included the fabric departments of well-known department stores.

We toured wholesale fabric houses to see the manufacturing process of making clothing for the retail market. Wholesale dress manufacturing procedures are set up for fast, efficient management. We watched a machine, which looked like a chainsaw, cut a large stack of fabric from a pattern. Buzzing, loud sewing machines in a hot, unpleasant, murky environment made me realize what a hard job it was to work in those factories.

As part of Avondale Mills' national marketing plan, Elizabeth Taylor was featured on the cover of the *Saturday Evening Post,* wearing a dress made from the Mills' chambray cloth. This design could never be sold in department stores, as it was made especially for the glamorous Hollywood actress, Elizabeth Taylor.

Our host planned a trip to a Broadway show where we saw Ethel Merman in *Annie Get Your Gun.* Mary Pickford, "America's Sweetheart," the queen of the silent movies, was recognized as being in the audience that night. The audience was excited she was there. We did other tourist-type things to complete our introduction to this new world of which we were now a part. New York City was Broadway and vibrant nightlife, while DC was old monuments and government buildings. I was thoroughly entranced with both. After this trip and the trips that followed, Ann, Frances, and I returned to our little mill in Sylacauga, Alabama, to design and create new fashions. It seemed we were forever designing and sewing garments.

The mill was constantly promoting its business. One of the largest events was the state fair in Birmingham. The design department was responsible for hosting and staging fashion shows at the fair. Over the course of the week, we put on several fashion shows daily. In addition, we put in long hours playing hostess at the exhibit and mingling with the fair crowds.

Finally Friday arrived, and Frances and I went back to our hotel after a busy week to get ready for our dinner dates. Buddy and his friend, Graham, who we called Slugger, came to Birmingham to see the show and to take me and Frances out to eat. They were late, and we were starving. I hated waiting and thought it was rude of them to keep us waiting. I was far too tired and worn out to be sociable once they finally arrived. We'd been "walking the runway" all day. In fact, the whole week had been demanding and overly exhausting. I felt so tired I refused to go out. The next morning, red roses were delivered to our room; they were for me. It was the only time I'd ever get roses from anyone. Buddy assured me Slugger was the problem with timing. I believed him but was still so tired it didn't improve my mood much. The state fair was always a challenging and exhausting experience for us. It got very old quickly.

The next big trip planned for us was to meet the Avondale Mills sales department in Chicago. We wore our fashions as usual and learned their marketing strategy. As in New York, we went to a large department store and enjoyed the local flavor of the town. We were treated to a meal at The Pump Room, a famous restaurant known for some of the country's best food and where celebrities and politicians frequently congregated. I ordered something that came to our table on a flaming sword. I think the Chicago salespeople especially enjoyed entertaining three southern girls who were seeing the Windy City for the first time.

Since we weren't delegated a specific hostess, we decided to see Tallulah Bankhead on our own. She was touring in *Private Lives*, and it was showing in a theatre in Chicago. We didn't call ahead to reserve tickets but took a taxi hoping it wasn't sold out. We should've known there'd be no chance of getting tickets. But I had a bright idea I thought might get us in. I told the box office person we were from Alabama and in Chicago for just a few days and that Tallulah Bankhead was also an Alabama girl, from Huntsville. I went on to explain that she was our former governor's daughter, whom we were very anxious to see in this special play. Luckily they made a place for the three of us to sit on a small bench along the back wall of the theater. I think it must've been the ushers' resting spot. Even so, we enjoyed the play. It was a whirlwind trip but so much fun!

Another *get acquainted* trip was to Dallas, TX, where we were involved in promotional activities. We had a large wardrobe of outfits made for us and for the models. Neiman Marcus, a prominent department store, was featuring a fashion show in their dry goods department. The store arranged for an inexperienced young man to provide models and help produce the show. His models didn't have the appearance nor skill of professional models, though, and it showed. It turned out we knew more about producing the show than he did. Afterwards, Ann, Frances, and I remained in the fabric department for two days, strolling around in our creations, talking with customers, and promoting the fabrics. This was far more successful than the clunky, unprofessional show the young man had produced.

During my off-work time, I decided to visit the beauty salon in Neiman Marcus. I asked the hairstylist to style my hair in a new, creative hairdo. He gave me the newest style. I got the real deal! A short, upswept style that was just then getting trendy. The stylish hairdo was good for my new role as a model/commentator for the fashion shows.

While passing through the lobby of the hotel we were staying at, there was a big commotion going on with cameras, reporters, and people gathered around. We saw a gentleman in the middle of the crowd, and everyone was listening intently to what he had to say. I later learned he was a pilot, Kenneth Arnold. He said he'd seen something he'd never seen before flying close to his plane. This was 1948, just as people were hearing about UFOs and flying saucers for the first time.

Back home at the Sylacauga home office, we were designing and making new outfits, traveling in a big bus with a wardrobe of garments hanging on racks. We took fashion shows throughout Alabama, going to clubs, stores, and special events as we promoted

69

our fabrics. We even wore our own outfits to festivals to promote our company products at those venues too.

On one trip we drove to Atlanta to show our clothing line at Rich's Department Store. When we flew back, we got home about the same time as we'd left Atlanta. That was odd—I wasn't aware of the different time zones. To me it seemed foolish for us to fly such a short distance, but then again, I've been frugal with money for as long as I've had any. A holdover from the Depression years, I guess.

Designing and creating new fashions and traveling to cities to show our clothing line was full of learning opportunities. I enjoyed four years helping to get the message out that Avondale Mills was moving on up by making fashion fabrics. So many new experiences that I never in my wildest dreams could've imagined.

This job was nothing like my OSS experience in any shape or form. My job at the mill was a creative process, where my individuality was appreciated. At OSS, I'd basically filed and kept records; there was nothing creative about it. In contrast, this job demanded creativity, and I was so happy to be able to show my own personal style and express my real self. I'd tapped into my creative side, and I liked it!

CHAPTER 16

———

Every Good Story
Has a Beginning

By the age of twenty-one, I'd already experienced a lifetime of memory-making experiences. But none of these would've happened if I'd not been born and raised in the household in which I was. My parents and grandparents formed my life's foundation, and I'll be forever grateful to them.

My mother and father met in 1923 in Dadeville, a small town in South Alabama. His name was Willard Milton Davis, but his friends just called him "Dave" or "Davis." He was the camp manager for Dixie Construction Company at the time, under contract with Alabama Power, installing new electrical lines throughout the state. The men set up camp in locations wherever they hung the lines. Periodically Daddy would ride his horse into Dadeville to conduct business and purchase supplies for himself and the workers. He'd pack his saddlebags with supplies the laborers needed, such as shaving soap, underwear, snacks, candy, etc. Once at camp, he'd unload those goods into a trunk, which served as a little store. His supplies were most welcomed by the men in the field who'd gather by the trunk to pick up provisions they needed.

On one of those visits to town, Daddy saw my mother, Una Belle Mahan, called "Cheatie," who was visiting her father working there. Daddy walked up to her and introduced himself and asked if he could walk her home. She was eighteen years old and a stunning young girl. They'd seen each other a few times in passing before that day, and he knew she was "Mr. Mahan's little girl." My mother accepted his request. After this, Mother and Daddy kept their friendship going by written correspondence and phone calls, and when he later visited her in her home, he sent her a telegram beforehand announcing his travel itinerary by train.

Mother was quite a musician. She played the piano beautifully, and Daddy played several instruments, too, including the saxophone. He also had a beautiful tenor voice. Daddy didn't bring her candy like other boyfriends; he always brought her sheet music when he came calling. "My Blue Heaven," "In the Good Ole' Summertime," "Ramona," "Pennies from Heaven," and other songs from that time were their favorites. That old sheet music always had a place on our piano alongside our recital music while I was growing up.

They courted a while and married in February 1925. Mother kept a picture of Daddy in her scrapbook where she'd drawn an arrow pointing to him and written, "A man after my own heart."

I was born on November 5th, 1925, right in the middle of the Roaring Twenties—a prosperous, celebrated time in America. My parents named me Peggy Mahan Davis. It was a new family's beginning.

World War I was over, and with a prosperous economy, it was like a big party. The Roaring Twenties were known for their outrageousness. Bobbed hair and short dresses were in style, and women were experiencing a renaissance—they could now vote, wear makeup, cut their hair, dress more provocatively, and work among men. New dances like the Charleston and the Lindy Hop were all the rage. Societal attitudes began to shift, leading to what many viewed as a decline in moral values.

Living in the Bible Belt, however, meant the southern states were slower to adapt to those new, *loose* standards, and life went on as usual. The stock market crash of 1929 brought on the Great Depression, resulting in hard times nationwide and a dampening of the Roaring Twenties' free-spiritedness. Although the South was largely unaffected by the cultural shift of the time, almost everyone's lifestyle was greatly affected by the market crash. Everyone was in for hard times. Jobs were extremely hard to come by, and families often became uprooted to go wherever there was work.

Daddy returned to his job in South Alabama, and Mother and I joined him a little later. Life went on as usual for the Davis family. After two years of living in several small towns in South Alabama, Mother and I returned to her hometown of Clanton to wait for the birth of her second child. On November 28th, 1927, another baby girl was born: my little sister, Una Faye. After Faye's birth, Mother and I settled down in Clanton while Daddy made the transition into another type of job with Alabama Power.

In 1928, we left Clanton and moved about an hour and a half's drive away to Gorgas, Alabama, where Alabama Power owned a steam plant that generated electricity. Daddy began working in the office. Grandma and Grandpa Mahan moved with us since Grandpa would be helping maintain Rattlesnake Dam.

They were all so excited to move into a newly built, company-owned house. Daddy was helping to bring high voltage lines to areas around the state. In the cities, most people had electric lights but little else that ran off electricity. Over the next several years, newfangled things such as radios, washing machines, vacuum cleaners, blenders, and whatnot were coming on the market for home use.

One day I watched a truck drive into our driveway, delivering an unusual-looking thing that Daddy said was going to wash all our clothes and the baby's diapers. (Apparently it was an unexpected birthday gift for Mother.) The entire neighborhood showed up in our yard, loud and excited like I was, asking questions about how this odd machine could wash clothes. My mother was the most excited, by far.

I was far too young to care that a wringer washing machine could turn pants pockets inside out, but I still remember all the excitement of the day. Many decades later, in 2003, when we went to sell my mother's house in Tuscaloosa, that very same Maytag washing machine was still in the basement. It had moved with her from place to place as one of Mother's prized possessions.

In 1929, after a short time living in Gorgas, we moved back to Clanton, Alabama, (again) to wait for Daddy's next assignment with the power company. This great house on the hill was a special place. It was Mother's childhood home, our getaway home, and the source of many of my childhood memories.

The house had a Victorian flair, with ornate gables, turrets, and a large porch that extended across the front of the house. There was a fireplace in each bedroom but no central heating or cooling. Each side room opened onto the porch, which made the summer nights cooler when the doors were propped open. The porch was the center of most of the activities at "The Hill," as we called it, and it was a fun place for us to play. Potted plants bloomed alongside the length of the porch, and multiple chairs were available for visiting neighbors. At the back of the porch was a washstand for family, workers, and guests to wash their hands before meals. Of course, there was no indoor running water in the early years at The Hill.

Our drinking well was right beside the side porch. The well was a major part of life for us; there was no other source of water. There's nothing quite as refreshing as cool spring water, and I learned early on as a small child to draw up the bucket from the depths of the well. A dried gourd dipper and a metal dipper with a long handle rested on the post beside the well. My child-length arms were short, and it was hard to get the dipper to my mouth without splashing water all over my clothes. But I'd rather be wet than thirsty, and it never took long for my clothes to dry in the intense summer heat.

Papa Mahan had a cabinet shop down the hill from Grandma's garden. Workers in his cabinet shop enjoyed the convenience of a water break during their workday. Customers to the shop, neighboring visitors, and kinfolk frequently stopped by our well on their way to town. It was a popular watering/gathering spot.

As we grew up, the backyard was like a playground for us. Playing with my cousin, Sara Charles, was the summer highlight for me. We didn't have a lot of store-bought toys; instead, we learned to entertain ourselves with our imaginations. When the weather permitted, we had lots of fun playing hide-and-seek, jump rope, Simon Says, and dodgeball, and we also created our own games. In inclement weather, we put on made-up plays or performances inside the house. The yard was our place to play, but the house was *not*. We could write and plan our plays, but we couldn't hold our theatrical performances inside the house. There were important rules for indoors: no running, no slamming the screen doors, no loud noise, and we could never say "shut up" to anyone. If an argument started, Grandma would say, "No multiplying words." Children of those times relied on their imagination and ingenuity for entertainment—so very different from children today.

In the twilight of the evenings, we'd go outside while the babies of the family were being put to bed. We'd quietly tell stories or get a jar and catch lightning bugs. It was fun to tie a string on a big june bug's leg and let the bugs fly around the yard. I have to admit, I did feel sorry for the poor little bugs and would take the strings off their legs after we'd flown them around a while.

On January 26th, 1930, Faye and I were playing in the sandbox as we watched the distinguished Dr. Gragg and his wife walk to the porch. Dr. Gragg was carrying his little black satchel, and he and his nurse-wife went through the bedroom door where Mother was "resting." We'd been told not to go in there that day, so we stayed in the yard. When Dr. Gragg and his wife left, we were told we had a little brother; his name was John Milton. How happy everybody seemed to be that we had a baby boy! In my mind, I assumed the baby had been brought into the house inside Dr. Gragg's satchel. Seemed quite a reasonable assumption (as a preschooler) to me.

We'd been in the Clanton house on The Hill for about six months when Daddy accepted a permanent assignment with Alabama Power in Shelby County. His office would be in Montevallo. The offer letter said, "Tell the little girls they will have a lot of pine straw to play in." Pines are commonplace in the South, and there were pine trees all around the house he'd rented. At least now we'd have some shade.

CHAPTER 17

Moving to Montevallo

Electricity was now becoming a vital part of the culture all over the state, and Daddy's job was new to Montevallo, a small town with a population of only 1,224 in the 1930s. The town was geographically right in the middle of Alabama and home to Alabama College. The college was founded in 1896 as a technical college for girls: Alabama Girls' Industrial School. This school was an innovative experiment in education, instructing young women to become teachers, bookkeepers, artists, musicians, dressmakers, telegraphers, and milliners (hat makers). In 1919, it was renamed Alabama College, and in 1923 it officially became Alabama College, State College for Women, offering a liberal arts degree. In addition, home economics classes provided opportunities for students to practice cooking and sewing and learn how to be a homemaker.

What was really different was that this college ran a laboratory school attended by children from Montevallo and neighboring towns. Here, student teachers had a real-life opportunity to hone their teaching skills with actual students. From kindergarten forward, my education was shaped by this new teaching approach of collaboration between college students and community pupils. The college brought commerce and economic growth to Montevallo, and Wilton (a railroad community) as well as Aldridge and Dogwood (coal mining communities) were also part of the early growth. (In 1956, Alabama College dropped "State College for Women" from their name when they became a co-ed college. Now, though, it's known as the University of Montevallo, and *US News and World Report* ranked it as a "College of Distinction" and one of the "Top 15 Best Public Regional Universities in the South in 2022–23.")

Our little family moved to Montevallo during the summer of 1929, into a small house that sat behind a big house on Highland Avenue. Our house was one block from the college, the high school, and the elementary school, which turned out to be perfect. My new baby brother, John, was six months old. Daddy hired a nurse (who wore a uniform!) to help Mother with the baby. I was five and in kindergarten, and Faye was a little younger. Daddy and Mother borrowed money to buy a farm about fifteen miles from us. This would be for our Davis grandparents, who, during those hard Depression years, were having financial problems. Many big, life-changing decisions were being made very fast.

One of my favorite memories is of the weekly horse-drawn ice wagon that came through town during summer months. Faye and I would wait on the porch until we heard the tinkling bell of the ice wagon. The ice man was friendly and quite entertaining. He would chisel out a block of ice from the massive block in the back of the wagon, and we'd get the leftover ice chips as a treat. Then he'd use a huge pair of steel tongs to carry the smaller ice block to the icebox on our little kitchen porch. We always looked forward to the ice man's visits, like my children looked forward to the ice cream truck in their day.

Mother and Grandma Mahan were my early teachers. My Bible teaching started when I was only three or four years old. I spent a lot of time with Grandma, who taught me from the Bible. I had an illustrated ABC book that I loved, and Mother was the one who taught me to write. She and our Sunday school teachers also taught me Bible stories I could understand. I learned the prayer I always said before going to sleep:

> *Now I lay me down to sleep*
> *I pray the Lord my soul to keep.*
> *If I should die before I wake*
> *I pray the Lord my soul to take.*

I didn't understand why I might die during the night, but the Lord would take care of my soul if I did.

Of course, I had a child's curiosity and asked many questions. My mind swirled with mysteries of wonder about the sun, moon, thunder, rain, hail, cows, chickens, Grandma's false teeth, and God. I learned two main concepts related to God and life: being *good* and being *bad*. God was *good*. The boogeyman was *bad*, roaming around in the dark. This was eye-opening to me, and I became scared to be bad and tried my hardest to be good. So many things were solidified in my mind during those formative years, but the foundation of knowing right from wrong and good from bad formed the bedrock on which the rest of my life was based.

Grandma's schooling time started with me sitting on the steps off of her back porch, just outside the kitchen. She had me memorizing John 3:16 while she churned her milk. She continued quoting parts of that verse, which is the basic message of the Bible. I repeated the words after her until she was sure I could say it by myself. I still remember the words, and now I also understand their teaching: "For God so loved the world that He gave his only begotten son, that whoever believes in him shall not perish, but have eternal life."

After I'd memorized the verse and learned to recite it, she took me with her to a big summer tent revival meeting. After his sermon, the preacher asked anyone who had a special scripture to stand and recite it. Some lady stood up and recited *my* verse, and I was so relieved, thinking I wouldn't have to recite anything at all. However, Grandma wasn't deterred. She stood me up on the wooden bench. I was petrified with anxiety but dutifully recited the verse, and I believe I made Grandma the happiest woman in the whole church. She liked to show off her grandbabies.

By 1931 we'd moved into a larger house on Middle Street, half a block from the corner with the only traffic light. This house was known as the "Carmichael House." It was larger than the one we'd been living in, and it had a sleeping porch across the back. I was now six years old and in the second grade. Faye and John were enrolled in Alabama College's child development class, where college women observed instructors as they conducted the children's classes. It was not only beneficial for the teachers and students; it was also basically a daycare service for mothers. A win-win for everyone!

Around 1935 we moved again, this time to a rental next to a farm with a cornfield and potato patch. We called it "Tater Patch House." This is when I learned to drive—at about thirteen. The house was a ways out of town on the road leading to the railroad community of Wilton. Mother was pregnant and a bit concerned that we had no close neighbors. Daddy often worked odd hours with the power company, especially during bad weather. During those times, he'd be called into work, taking him away from the family.

Mother decided to teach me to drive our Model A Ford as a backup in case of an emergency. As the oldest, she was depending on me to drive her to the doctor, just in case. We first had to fold the back of the driver's seat down for me to sit on so I could see over the steering wheel. It was hard for my feet to reach the pedals, but we managed. To this day, I vividly remember that driving lesson, although I never got to drive that Model A car until I got my learner's permit. Gas was rationed, and the car stayed parked in the yard most of the time.

While living in the Tater Patch House, Mother returned to her childhood home in Clanton to have another baby. The baby was another boy, named Roy Watkins after Mother's brother. As I grew up, it seemed my mother was always growing babies. One day, Mother told me to get her recipe book. There was something in it about children—the "facts of life" about a baby's being in the mother's stomach. She wanted me and Faye to read about how babies were born. She didn't want to talk about it, she just wanted us to read it. We did.

Daddy eventually purchased us an inexpensive house. This was the first house that wasn't a rental. It was close to school and just three houses from Shoals Creek. Our family settled in this house for the rest of my early childhood. During that time, Mother gave birth to two more boys: Paul and, around three years later, Hubert, who we sometimes called Hugh.

CHAPTER 18

The Big Storm

It was noon on April 11th, 1939. I was thirteen years old, and that specific day will always stand out in my memory. I was at the college just finishing band practice in Palmer Hall. It was pouring down rain, and the skies were eerily dark, so we sat around to wait out the storm. Somebody said, "Peggy, sing us a song." So I sang, "Ah, Sweet Mystery of Life," and we passed the time with more singing. I was enjoying this showtime atmosphere.

When we decided the rain had cleared, we started strolling back to our high school. It was now lunch break, and my school friends saw me coming. They ran to hug me and told me my house had just been hit by a storm. I was in shock and scared out of my wits. We rushed into the high school building just as the intercom was calling me to come to the office for a phone call.

Daddy was calling me, calmly telling me not to come home for lunch that day. He seemed unemotional and was speaking very slowly, explaining, "There's been a bit of wind that damaged our house. Lines are down all over the ground. It's very dangerous. Nobody's hurt. Mother and the little ones are at Doctor Acker's (our neighbor's) house." I began crying and was already convinced there must've been more than "a bit of wind." I was thinking it must've been a really bad storm. I came out of the school office in tears. Friends gathered around me, asking questions, hugging me, and expressing their sympathy.

The band member who'd asked me to sing earlier shouted out to me, "It's a good thing you were singing for us and not with the angels." That was a sad thought for me, as I was thinking about my mother and little brothers in our wrecked house. Immediately I ran from the high school all the way home, stopping at Doctor Acker's house to hug Mother and hear her story. She was still in shock as she told me what had happened.

Talking rapidly, her words tumbled out: "It was pitch black, dark as night and very still. Then there was a loud noise like a train." She'd recognized those warning signals—a tornado! The bathroom was in the middle of the house and away from any windows. Her plan was to put Paul, baby Hubert, and Roy (almost five) in the bathtub. Wayne, who had stayed home from kindergarten with a fever, was in the big bed in the front bedroom. Mother picked him up to carry him to the bathroom too. As she came out of the front bedroom with Wayne in her arms, she could feel the floor moving as she stepped through the door. Just as she got into the bathroom, the loud noise was moving on. She put Wayne in the tub with the others. The next thing she could remember was rushing to the phone as the wind subsided a bit. She was in the hall just inside the front door trying to call Daddy when he came bursting in and grabbed her into his arms.

What a picture in my mind of my parents there in the old hallway, all wet and terrified and so thankful to be safe and alive. What a devastating story. Poor Wayne had nightmares for years after that, waking up screaming, "Don't let that wall fall on me!"

I wanted to see the damage to our house, so I left Mother at Doctor Acker's. Stepping carefully to avoid wires on the ground, I could see our house. As I got closer, I noticed that a neighbor's house diagonally across the street was totally flat, but most of the house was blown into our yard. I saw a blue wall first, then about three feet away bits and pieces of the rest of the wall were stuck under our Model A car. The car had obviously been lifted by the wind high enough for debris to blow up under the chassis. What a sight! Daddy told us later that one of his linemen climbed into the car, turned the motor on, and drove it off that mound of trash. That Model A was a tough old car!

The front roof of our house was gone. I went inside to check the damage. The walls and ceilings were still intact. I saw glass shards standing straight up in the pie on the kitchen table. Glass was scattered over the entire dining room, including the table of hot food that'd been set out for Daddy's lunch. A three- or four-foot splinter of blue wood pinned a bedroom curtain to the ceiling in the front bedroom where Wayne had been sick in bed. The floor of the sleeping porch was lifted up enough for a long piece of flooring to be threaded under it. I walked in water with trash everywhere, but amazingly the inside of the house wasn't damaged structurally.

I got my little Kodak Brownie camera the company had given to fifth-grade students years before and took some pictures. My pictures were used in a few of the local newspapers. The Alabama Power Company's newsletter also used my photos in a special edition about the storm, our house, and how Daddy had managed to efficiently restore power service to all of Shelby County. I was so proud of my daddy; he'd taken care of his family *and* helped the community get back on its feet.

We moved to Wilton while Papa Mahan and his carpenters began to renovate our house. As they inspected the damaged front section, they found a fireplace and flue in the chimney above the ceiling of our living room, confirming the house had originally been a two-story structure. A tornado years earlier had taken off the top of the original house. Old-timers in the town told us about another large house across the street that was destroyed during that other storm, leaving only the farmworker's house behind it where our neighbors now lived.

The new renovation included making our house a two-story once again, with two bedrooms upstairs. We spent a lot of our playing time helping refinish old furniture for our "new" home. Mother and Daddy told us the insurance company totally paid for this house renovation. I thought Papa Mahan's paternal love for his special daughter and her little ones made that insurance money work out just right.

Papa Mahan's brother, my Uncle Zed, kept his cabinet shop open that summer and made a cedar bedroom suite for me and Faye. We would soon have our own private room upstairs with new furniture. John and Willard, the two older boys, would have their own room across the hall from us.

We were able to move back into our renovated house just before school started that fall of 1939. We were all so much happier in our fixed-up house with the big bedrooms.

CHAPTER 19

My Growing Up Years

Living in Montevallo began a new life for our close-knit family. In fact, my entire life has been influenced by the role I had as the oldest of eight children. I was given responsibility for the others at a very young age. I remember when I was four, Mother let me take my two-year-old sister for a little walk, saying, "Take care of Una Faye. Hold her hand tightly." Soon I had baby brothers for my real dolls. Right then, I became "Little Mother" who could do so many helpful things for the babies.

As the years passed, more little brothers blessed our family until there were six of them. I assisted with all of their daily needs as we got older. My sister and I were often in charge of the smallest children who needed the most constant attention. Mother usually put me in charge of Roy. He was the inquisitive child of the bunch who had to be watched closely lest his curiosity get him in trouble. I learned the skills of childcare at a young age and enjoyed my family immensely. To me, family was pretty much everything, and that feeling stayed with me throughout my life.

Our parents would regularly go off for the evening to check on their parents. During those Depression years, that trip was also for getting milk, eggs, and other produce the grandparents shared with us. I'd be left in charge on those occasions. One time, John, the oldest boy, decided to challenge my authority. He wanted to leave the house for some reason, and I told him he couldn't do that. He yelled, "You can't tell me what to do. You're not my mother," as he hit the wall with his fist. He knew as well as I did that he was responsible for following our family's rules. The oldest boy was part of the chain of command for his young brothers. Thankfully John didn't hurt his fist when he hit the wall, but it scared me half to death.

I remember my growing up years like they were yesterday. The kitchen and dining room were the hub of family life, and mealtime was always a special time. When the whole family was together for meals, we never started eating until everything was ready and every family member was sitting at the table. The seating order was established: as the oldest, I was just to the right of Daddy on the girls' bench. John, as the oldest boy, was to the left of Daddy on the boys' bench. The silly, most giggling brother on the boys' bench was usually moved to the girls' bench. In our big family, this kind of order was expected.

After the food was on the table and everyone was seated, Daddy always prayed his prayer, the *thank-you blessing*. He'd recite it ever-so-slowly and deliberately, and we were all hanging on every word, just waiting for the "Amen!" The boys usually began squirming toward the end of the really long prayers.

Often the plates were stacked at the head of the table in front of Daddy. He'd serve each plate and pass it around as we all waited patiently. During those hard times, Daddy wanted to make sure we weren't being wasteful (or overly greedy). There was always a roast on Sunday, and Daddy would cut up the meat portion for each child and add vegetables before passing it to him or her. When all were served, we'd start eating. As we ate, we could ask for second helpings as long as we said "please." If there was any leftover roast, Mother would grind it up, and we'd add mayonnaise to it for lunch sandwiches. Meal prep for a family of ten takes up a lot of time, and it seemed I was forever making sandwiches!

Daddy was a stickler for good manners, especially at the table. Besides table manners, he schooled us on our behavior in general as we discussed our day-to-day life. During dinner conversation, someone usually tattled on somebody else (as children are prone to do), but good events were shared with everyone, and there was plenty of laughter mixed in.

Luckily, we didn't have too many family emergencies. One time, though, Mother and the baby came to see me perform in a school musical, leaving Faye in charge. The older boys were teaching younger brother, Wayne, to ride the only bicycle we owned. Wayne was *constantly* begging to ride the bicycle. The boys decided to start the lesson by having Wayne coast downhill. He ended up in a ditch with a bloody head injury. His guilty older brothers rushed him home to Faye, who immediately called Daddy at his office. When Daddy and Faye got Wayne to the doctor's office for stitches, Daddy was about to faint. Daddy, our giant, our hero! The nurse sat him down and gave him something on a piece of cotton to calm his nerves. We'd never seen Daddy like this, but he quickly recovered and redeemed his hero status. It was a dramatic experience for us all.

When they got home with Wayne all bandaged up, a very impressive greeting was waiting for them. The four guilty, frightened, sorrowful boys were in the living room, standing on the stairs, singing, "Happy get well to Wayne. Happy get well to Wayne." But they had to stop their made-up song because they were crying so hard. Each boy had a gift for Wayne too. Big brother John had instructed the boys to each give Wayne their favorite toy. John gave him a toy he'd made, Willard gave him his *Big, Little* book (a popular book the children shared), and Roy gave him some marbles. But young Paul had no toy of his own, so he gave Wayne some peanut butter and crackers.

On nights when Daddy would come home for supper after we'd already eaten, Mother would tell me to take the boys for a walk "so Daddy can eat in peace." I think she wanted her own special time with Daddy during a quiet evening meal.

In the summer, we'd often go to the school playground. We lived near the Little Springs picnic area where there was a great swimming hole, and we often went there for picnics. When the weather was nice, I enjoyed taking the boys there with soap and towels in hand for a soapy swim instead of a long walk. The boys especially liked this, preferring it over the usual nightly group bath in the tub at home. When we went for walks, usually a bit of running was involved along the way. Faye called them "running walks," and she didn't care for them at all. Faye usually stayed at home when we did those, but I loved to run as much as those boys.

As the family grew with each new baby, my status as the big sister and Mother's helper was reinforced. I taught my little brothers nursery rhymes and Bible stories. At bedtime, I read books to them. I helped them learn to crawl, walk, count, and say their ABCs. I even used the same ABC book Mother had used to teach me. Some of the games I played with the boys were kick-the-can and baseball (with only one base and a board bat). I taught them how to catch lightning bugs and make kites and slingshots. And, as I grew older, like a parent, I attended their special school programs.

My most important duty was being in full charge of the family when Mother and Daddy would go to Clanton to check on Mother's parents. They'd usually go weekly to get milk, eggs, and sometimes vegetables. Sometimes we all went with them and stopped by the farm to say hello to our Davis grandparents. Often when we visited, Daddy and his parents would have "a fun family music time" with Papa Davis leading the group and playing his guitar. Grandma Davis and Daddy played the mandolins, and when Uncle Paul was there, he played the violin. Mother, Faye, the boys, and I would sing the old familiar songs, "America the Beautiful," "In the Good Old Summertime," "Dixie," and "My Blue Heaven." We all looked forward to those get-togethers.

CHAPTER 20

The World Around Me

The Great Depression (1929–1941) came a few years after I was born. The economic conditions that caused a world disaster are well documented; however, my little Montevallo hometown was not drastically affected like the agricultural and manufacturing communities were. Our small college was the main source of income for many of the residents. My daddy was involved with providing the electrical services for the entire county, so his income was secure, but unemployment was the entire country's major problem.

As a child, the way of life brought on by this national crisis was just our normal life. Everybody was affected by it. Our lives functioned around the urgent necessity to be thrifty, creative, helpful, and united as a community and a culture. Our country's motto during that time was, "Use it up. Wear it out. Make do, or do without!" That frugal philosophy remains a principle of my life today. I wash and reuse plastic bags. I save string. I keep bottles. I reuse boxes. I wear old clothes. In my mind, it's wasteful to throw things in the garbage that can be used in any other way.

Our family fit into this pattern, as we all had responsibilities and jobs in the community. The older boys delivered groceries or the local newspaper and worked in the print shop or at the movie theater. Faye and I had many babysitting jobs, and in high school I had a typing job in the principal's office.

I was even the designated family barber for my brothers. The boys would sit on the post in the backyard, which was the base for our fun whirly jig (a homemade copy of a fancy playground ride). I used clippers to cut their hair, but it was hard to manipulate the clunky clippers because of my small hands. The boys screamed and complained that I purposely pulled their hair out by the roots with those clippers. Actually, the clippers were just very dull and inefficient. The scissors were less painful and did a very good job.

I also learned to sew from Grandma Mahan on her Singer pedal sewing machine. I made all my own clothes plus some things for the other children and continued doing this until I was grown.

In our family, shoes were worn by several members as we kids grew up. When water leaked into the holes in the soles, Daddy got out his pocketknife and cut out a cardboard inner sole for the shoes. Later when he could afford the expense, he'd tell us to stop by the town shoe shop and get new soles. I remember sitting and watching a cute teenage boy fix my shoes one day. (His father owned the mechanic shop, and the shoe shop was attached to it.) This schoolboy used my Daddy's pattern to cut out new leather soles and a big sewing machine to stitch them onto the shoes like a pro.

To me, this was like a fascinating craft project demonstration. He even polished the shoes, and I got new shoestrings to complete my "new" shoes. I couldn't have been happier with a brand-new pair. Mother called a local shoe salesman who'd come to our house when our family needed real new shoes. He'd order a well-made, quality brand that was intended to be worn until they literally wore out. There was no artificial leather at that time. There was also no shoe store in our town, just a general merchandise store that sold poor quality shoes for children.

One of the ways I knew trouble was brewing for other people during those times was the prevalence of hobos. I was curious about those men who'd lost their jobs and were traveling on freight trains in boxcars, looking for work. Our home was near the railroad that provided their free travel. The hobos needed meals while they traveled, so they'd knock on our side dining room door, usually near mealtime, wanting food. Mother always fixed them something, but she usually asked them to chop some kindling, or she handed them an empty coal scuttle to bring in some coal while she filled their plate with good, hot, healthy food.

Daddy told us the hobos knew where to come for a good meal. He said they had their own code for leaving messages for other hobos. There were several terms related to their lifestyle. People would say to friends, "Hop a freight and come see us sometime!" *Riding the rails* and *rail runners* were hobo terms familiar to me as a child.

On our trips to see our grandparents, the highway followed the train tracks along the way, and we'd play a game to see how many hobos we saw. We liked to wave to them to see which ones would wave back. It was cheap amusement for children like us who had to be creative with our fun activities. Very different car entertainment was needed for children in later decades, but it worked back then.

Sometimes there would be a chain gang working along US Route 31 to Clanton. Daddy said they were trustee prisoners chained together in a working line along the highway. They wore black and white uniforms. A rifleman guarded them so they wouldn't run away. We'd wave at them, but they didn't wave back.

We obtained one of the new major inventions that became available to the public during this Depression era. The most exciting Christmas event for our family was the year Daddy surprised us all, even Mother.

On Christmas morning, 1935, we rushed into the living room to the tree to see what Santa Claus had brought us. Suddenly, Daddy left the room. In a little while we heard loud Christmas music coming from the main bedroom, which was like our family room during the winter since it was the warmest. The big living room had a Ben Franklin coal stove and was only used on weekends and special occasions. (We didn't want to waste coal in rooms that weren't used during school days.)

Hearing the loud music, we all raced to the bedroom. The door was locked. Daddy had locked the door and only opened it when he was sure we were all patiently waiting. He had purchased a radio! It was to stay in that main bedroom, and it became an important part of our lives. The radio was the major communication invention since the telephone, which had been around since Mother was a young girl.

Kids bundled up at Grandma Mahan's

Kids in the yard

Peggy (age 3)

OSS building

OSS memorial medallion

Portrait of Peggy

Look Magazine - tanning on a boat

Look Magazine - on the beach

Look Magazine article

Look Magazine - sailing

Modeling shot of Peggy (R)

Newspaper article on Peggy

Modeling shot of Peggy

Peggy at the pool in Montevallo

Modeling shot of Peggy

Peggy in Mt. Vernon

Peggy in Mt. Vernon with Tall John and Williard

Peggy and Milly outside their apartment

Buddy and Peggy:
King and Queen of Cotton

Peggy on 42nd Street in NYC

Peggy in NYC

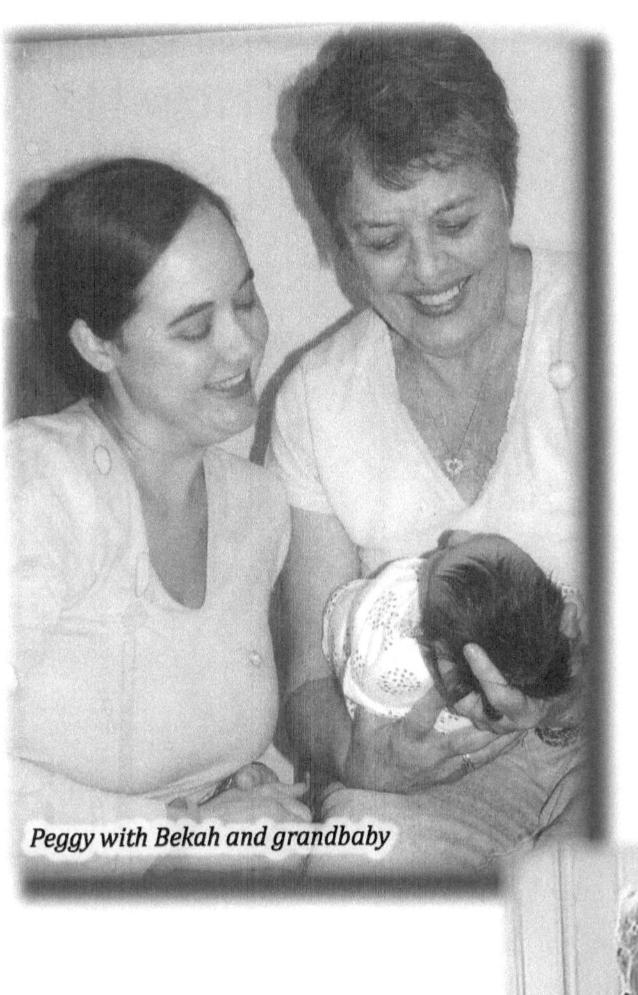

Peggy with Bekah and grandbaby

Peggy

CHAPTER 21

President Roosevelt and the New Deal

Even though I was just a preteen, I heard enough news on that radio about our President Roosevelt and his New Deal. The New Deal was a series of programs, public work projects, financial reforms, and regulations enacted by President Franklin D. Roosevelt between 1933 and 1939. Those programs were for men who were out of work, which was intended to help the United States out of the Depression. The president's New Deal definitely impacted our Depression years. There was even a painting in our US Post Office by artists of the Federal Art Project (FAP). Our class went to watch the artists while they were working on it.

Papa Mahan's nephew, a cabinet shopworker, got a job with the Civilian Conservation Corps (CCC), which was designed to supply jobs for young men and to relieve families who had difficulty finding jobs during the Depression years. This program was one of the most successful of the New Deal programs. Buddy's sister, May Lyman Woods, went to work with the Tennessee Valley Authority

(TVA) as a secretary for a while right after finishing college. She liked living in the summer-camp-style mountain cabins built for the employees.

The most important New Deal program was Social Security, which, as we all know, is still in effect today. Even though I couldn't understand the meaning of the political and economic grownup talk, I realized even then that the Social Security program was important for our future welfare as a nation. I heard the term *old folks' homes* and knew that was where some of my grandmother's friends and acquaintances lived.

Years earlier, my second grade *Weekly Reader* newspaper had posted articles about Roosevelt's election in 1933. He remained president all my young life until he died in 1945. He was an important and popular leader during his four consecutive terms as president. We never missed listening to his informative Fireside Chats on our home radio. When Roosevelt came on, we knew to be calm, quiet, and serious because whatever he was saying was obviously very important to Mother and Daddy.

Grandma Mahan was a strong pioneer woman of the late 1800s. She knew about farm life. She told me stories about their big house with a weaving room and a potato cellar, her chores in the vegetable garden as a child, their one-room school, and the *Blue Back Speller* and *McGuffey Readers* that were her principal schoolbooks.

When I was a little girl, Grandma Mahan and many other townsfolk planted and maintained large gardens like the ones they'd worked on as youngsters. When Grandma's garden was in full harvest, our family helped with the canning process. This was a way of life for many during the early 1900s, and it surely helped our big family through the Depression. Many people didn't have food, but we were lucky to have a working daddy and grandparents who helped us in many ways. Home canning is now a lost art. Food processing is done in factories, but there will never be better food than the canned vegetables and fruits we put up for the winter when I was a child.

Preparation was the first task in the canning process. There were vegetables to be picked, green beans to be snapped, peas to be shelled, cucumbers to be primed for pickles, spices to be added; there was fruit to be peeled, corn to be shucked, firewood to be gathered, water to be drawn from the well, and labor to be invested to prepare the harvest.

Truckloads of pears were harvested from Papa's property near Mobile, Alabama, for our families and bartered with kinfolk and friends for peaches and apples. We picked figs from the bush near the porch washstand for my favorite treat: fig preserves. Grandma even knew secret places to go in the nearby woody area near town to get blackberries and blueberries. We helped pick berries with old socks covering our arms to protect us from red bug bites and briars.

I thought helping with the canning was a lot of fun. Grandma said my little hands could get down inside the big quart mason jars better than anybody's. I would compete with other young helpers to see who could wash the most jars or shell the most peas or peel the most pears or peaches. We even had a hand-operated peeler that made the job easy. We took turns cranking the peach peeler because we all thought it was fun. Then we'd use a knife to peel, making it a game to see who could do it in only one long peeling.

This efficiently orchestrated canning process was carried on in the hot kitchen and on the back porch, or in the yard just past the porch at the fancy washhouse area, using the big, black, wrought iron washpot. The jars had to be sterilized in boiling water in that big pot. Papa made some sort of fishnet gadget for handling the hot jars. I don't know how we tolerated the tremendous heat, which was necessary for cooking on that good old woodstove in the kitchen, or the blazing fire under the big washpot. Since the canning was taking place right there in the yard, the little children were cared for in a safer area as the work continued. That job was always shared by the older sisters. "Just keep your eyes on them," Mother would say. It was a big, hot, busy time.

The washpot at the washhouse in Grandma's yard was also used to make lye soap. There was no liquid soap, dishwashing soap, or window washing soap, nor were there any fancy soap bars. At Grandma's house, lye soap was used for all cleaning needs: on the porch handwashing shelf; in the bathtub; for washing clothes, towels, and sheets on the big washday; and for scrubbing floors. We didn't wash the floors; we scrubbed them.

This creative, frugal lifestyle of the 1930s was necessary for fulfilling our family's basic needs. However, it was also preparing us for the war years that had already begun in Europe. During the Great Depression, our country survived the worst economic crisis the nation had ever known. Those experiences set a good, strong foundation for life ahead. I was well prepared.

CHAPTER 22

Progressive Education

The early years of my life were intricately connected to Alabama College. Alabama was part of a nationwide program centered around *progressive education*, a new approach to teaching. With this approach, more value was given to experiences than to formal learning. The goal was to concentrate on the development of the child's talents. Throughout school, our grades were either marked as *U* for unsatisfactory or *S* for satisfactory. Classes were organized with *model* teachers and *student* teachers, and both were involved in presenting lessons. At times, an entire class of college students came into our classroom and observed the class and our teachers. When the college student teachers taught a class, they were always monitored. There was never a shortage of teachers growing up.

At sixth-grade graduation, we were given a certificate issued from the Alabama College Teacher Training School. It was a big day for us. I'd been chosen to lead the audience, singing, "The Star-Spangled Banner" and reciting the "Pledge of Allegiance" to the American flag. During this time, I became more aware of our connection to our community as well as to the college. When we were learning about our country, our state, or our town, we talked about the different kinds of stores, services, and jobs. Merchants representing jobs and services in Montevallo visited our classes to tell us about their jobs. Daddy was the volunteer fire chief at the time, and he brought the firetruck so we could see it firsthand.

I was introduced to basic music lessons by a college professor and her students during my early school grades. We had piano lessons and we had rhythm bands for reading music. When I was twelve, my class received an invitation from Mr. Kildea, the high school band director and a college professor, to take instrumental lessons so we would be ready for the high school band. My sister, Faye, and I took piano lessons from a local teacher, so Mr. Kildea suggested I also learn how to play the clarinet. Daddy bought one for me, and I was able to take lessons from a student teacher at the college.

While I was still in elementary school, the national Girl Scout program decided to add younger girls, and those girls would be called *Brownies*. I was part of the first Brownies group in Montevallo. Our mothers had to make uniforms for us that followed a specific pattern. I think the main purpose for us as Brownies was to be helpers and to learn about becoming Girl Scouts. We were helpers in making cookies and selling them, and before the US entered World War II, our Brownie troop was already knitting sweaters for the British troops. We were "Knittin' for Britain." In high school, I was a Senior Service Scout during the WWII years. During the warm summer months, our Girl Scout troop was taught swimming and diving skills by practice teachers from the college, and we could achieve badges. I received Red Cross certificates for junior lifesaving, senior lifesaving, and swim instructor training. These great experiences enriched my entire life.

Many veteran teachers attended summer school at the college to renew their certifications, and there was a need for students in their laboratory school for these classes. Local students were encouraged to attend in the morning during the early summer session. We had the privilege of attending a teacher-scheduled swim time in the college pool in the afternoons. This motivated us to attend the summer program. In fact, my family members always attended school in the summer, which left me only a few weeks of total freedom from school each year.

Mathematical skills have always been a hurdle for me, but in the third grade I was the first student in class to memorize the multiplication tables. As a reward, the teacher let me go out to the playground and sit under a tree and read during number study time. I look back with wonder that I ever got that recognition.

In the fourth grade my class planted two trees on the front lawn of the elementary school's campus for Arbor Day. We planned a real ceremony with a class speaker. We dug, planted, watered, and nurtured our trees. I regularly checked the growth of the trees for years while living in Montevallo.

In our town we also celebrated a holiday called Poppy Day as a symbolic remembrance for World War I veterans and victims. As I grew into young adulthood, I began to understand family, town, city, state, nation, world, and universe, and how they were all related. Many basic concepts were part of related practices that began as early as my elementary school years. The Pledge of Allegiance, singing the National Anthem, prayer time, and learning about and participating in holiday ceremonies and civic activities were common practices.

After sixth grade, my class crossed the elementary school campus once a week to visit the high school's library. Grades seven, eight, and nine were junior high, and ten, eleven, and twelve were considered senior high. Many neighboring schools only went to the eleventh grade. High school buses started to bring more and more students to our school from nearby coal mining and railroad communities.

In high school, the class format and focus was different from the structured elementary classes. We had fewer student teachers observing or practicing teaching in our classes. Probably fewer wanted to teach older adolescent students. However, we always had physical education practice teachers that worked with us under the supervision of the high school coach.

Although we had regular classwork such as math, English, and social studies, we also had a long, midday class called the *integrated period* where we each chose our special interests and explored those interests with our own individualized activities. I quickly chose art and music, and my learning was focused on those interests. I had the awesome opportunity of attending several days of a college harmony and ear training class where I learned about the sound formation and progression of different musical chords.

Our learning in math and English progressed mostly using workbooks, so we moved through at our own pace without any real hardcore learning. I was hit hard in English 101 later in college because of my lack of formal drills and memorization of grammatical knowledge in my younger school years. Mother was shocked that I didn't know how to diagram a sentence, and there was little homework or memorization in high school. In our homerooms, we discussed current events and created projects that correlated to those news events. During WWII we discussed where the European countries involved in the war were located, but we had no formal geography lessons. Our school projects included experiences related to the war effort, like our project to collect scrap iron used to make ammunition for the Allied troops. I was very happy with the wonderful opportunities I had in the college's laboratory school, but my parents were much less enthusiastic.

Looking back, I realize now how fortunate I was to have had so many hands-on, unique learning opportunities. I visited Miss Allen in the college's pottery shop. She was my Brownie and Girl Scout leader and also my elementary art teacher. Under her guidance, I learned how to work with clay and use the pottery wheel, and I happily became involved with drawing and painting. I was selected to create a large drawing for the bulletin board, showing familiar monuments in France such as the Eiffel Tower, the Arc de Triomphe, and Notre Dame. It was a class team effort. My job mostly entailed drawing with students and helping to paint our big masterpiece.

Although we had math classes, my education did not include a good foundation in math, and I had no natural inclination nor interest in that subject. When I was in eighth grade, an important visiting research professor came to our classroom. We were told he was from some big "university up north" and to be on our best behavior. It was exciting to know that he'd come just to see our school. He asked how many of us were studying algebra. I raised my hand, sitting there in the front row, and he pointed directly to me and asked, "Why are you taking algebra, young lady?" I wondered why I was taking it myself but instinctively came up with what I thought was a *cute* answer. Smiling, I said, "Oh, just to exercise my brain, I guess."

Daddy was my helper when I had math homework, which was rare. He hadn't stayed in high school to get his diploma. He said, "I learned all they had to teach me." Eventually he did attend a business college in Poughkeepsie, New York. My mother had taken four years of Latin, and she excelled at grammar. She knew all about diagramming sentences. She enjoyed being involved in community spelling bees, and she often quoted poems and read and analyzed classical literature in her school years.

My parents didn't like many things about the way we were being educated. We never received report cards showing our grades and progress. Instead, we'd get a written essay of our progress. My parents, and other parents too, thought this practice was radical and random. My brother Willard received a written essay-type report card, and I heard my parents discussing their concerns about it. The teacher had praised him for being a well-adjusted child and well-liked by other students, "especially the little girls." Daddy was apprehensive about that kind of evaluation. Years later, his goal was to move his six, good-looking boys away from that "girls' college town." At age fifteen, Willard was already attracting attention and receiving phone calls from the college girls. Meanwhile, my youngest brother, Hubert, was praised in his kindergarten report for cleaning up a spill without being told what to do. This had nothing to do with his aptitude, and I'm sure my parents had a hard time adjusting to that new teaching strategy so radically different from their own.

CHAPTER 23

———————

My Buddy

My childhood, high school, and college years were filled with wonderful experiences and the wonders of living in a small town in the South, where everyone knew everyone else. It was a more innocent time in a more innocent place, and those ingrained values remained with me throughout my life. My roots were in Montevallo, and that's also where I met my future husband, Buddy Woods.

Buddy's mother's family, the Lymans, was a prominent family that had initially lived in Connecticut. In the late 1800s, Buddy's maternal grandfather moved his family south and helped establish the small town of Montevallo, Alabama. The Lymans were both socially and politically active in the town throughout the time of my childhood. Judge Lyman was the county judge and mayor of Montevallo. When I was in the fourth grade, he visited my class and talked about the town's history. He told us the name came from the Cherokee Indians who described the area as "mountain-valley," and *Montevallo* was a derivative of that.

The Lyman family owned a big house across the street from Alabama College. Buddy was born in that house, and he started school in Montevallo, but his family later moved to Fort Mill South Carolina.

In 1939, Buddy's father died suddenly at age fifty-one from a cerebral hemorrhage, and the family was devastated. Buddy's mother, Laura Lyman Woods ("Miss Laura," as we all called her), brought her daughter, Frances, back to the Lyman House in Montevallo, but Buddy stayed behind to finish his college classes at Clemson.

After moving back to Montevallo, Miss Laura planned a huge Lyman family reunion. She called my mother and asked if she could "borrow one of those cute little boys" to play with her grandson. I'd met Frances at school, and her cousin Robert, "Obbie," had been my steadfast friend since kindergarten. As planned, on the day of the reunion, I took one of my little brothers over to the Lyman House, and that was when I met Buddy for the first time. He'd driven over from Fort Mill in his Model A car, "Lilly Belle"—a convertible with a rumble seat. Several of us piled in, and Buddy took us for a ride in Lilly Belle. I was about fifteen, and even though Buddy was twenty-two, he was more than happy to entertain the younger ones and show off his car. What I noticed the day I first met Buddy was how friendly and gracious he was to everyone, especially his mother, and his kindness impressed me. His father would've been very proud of him, I thought.

Our "gang," as Mother called my teenage group of friends, often met for hangouts at the Lyman House. It was our meeting place for Monopoly, cards, gossip, and whatever else we could come up with. Buddy brought Frances a record player for her birthday one year, as he would drive down for special occasions (holidays, birthdays, etc.) in Jeannie, his car after Lilly Belle. Our paths crossed occasionally.

Buddy graduated from Clemson in 1941 when he was twenty-three, receiving a diploma in textile engineering. In addition, because he'd been enrolled in the Army Air Force Reserve Officer Training Corps (ROTC), he received his military orders. He got his Officer Wings in 1942 and reported for military duty. During this time, he left Jeannie at the Lyman House for Frances, Obbie, and his mother to use. I even dated Obbie in that car.

Buddy wanted to be a pilot, but vision issues prevented him from doing so. He served in the Air Force at Geiger Field in Spokane, Washington, and the Pocatello Army Air Base in their navigational training department in Pocatello, Idaho. He excelled in his navigational training class and became a navigational instructor. He taught celestial navigation, which uses the sky (stars, planets, and the sun and moon) rather than instrumentation, but his heart really wasn't in it. He wanted to fly. He finally did get to fly as a navigator on a B-24 Liberator heavy bomber, and he loved it. He served active duty in the Pacific Theater during World War II and flew thirty-two dangerous missions.

Buddy couldn't visit the Lyman House as much then, but he frequently wrote to his mother. Our gang still hung out there, and occasionally Miss Laura read his letters aloud to us. We looked forward to those letters, full of intrigue, imagining what our soldiers must be experiencing halfway across the world. We lived vicariously through Buddy, and he was our hero.

After the war, Buddy returned home. He started working at Avondale Mills and had been living and working there in Sylacauga for about a year since his return to civilian life. We'd gotten to know each other and had been corresponding since my college's senior prom. He'd send me letters addressed to "Miss Peggy," which my brothers found quite amusing. When I finally got the job at the mill, Buddy came to get me for the hour's drive to Sylacauga. As he was putting my luggage in his car, Mother said, "Buddy, take good care of Miss Peggy over there in Sylacauga." He never forgot it and reminded me of it often.

Immediately I began to adjust to a new life, new exciting experiences, and new friends. My coworker, Frances Weaver, and I became roommates in the Big House on Main Street, which was a boarding house. We ate meals at Maggie Bell's house around the corner from the boarding house. The tables there were set up in the living room for around twenty people to eat evening meals. Buddy and his two friends, with whom he shared a garage apartment, also ate their evening meal there after work. These daily meetings were like a party, as we were usually the first group there. Buddy and I felt comfortable with each other; we enjoyed being friends. A few times we went to movies in Childersburg after dinner because there wasn't a lot to do in Sylacauga.

A few weeks after I got settled in my new surroundings, Buddy asked if I'd like to see my family and their new home in Tuscaloosa. Of course, I was anxious to do just that. It was so thoughtful of him to ask. My parents had patiently waited for me to finish college and move out of the house, and Daddy had to find just the right house before they made their big move. He had a new job with the Alabama Power Company, and this was his opportunity to move their six, good-looking boys away from the girls' college.

In late August of 1947, Buddy and I drove to Tuscaloosa to check out my parents' new house. I was so thrilled for the family to begin this new chapter of their lives in a larger house than the one in Montevallo. I was also very glad for them to get better acquainted with Buddy.

The Davis family's new house was *big*. On the first floor were three bedrooms, a big living room, a dining room, a breakfast nook, a large kitchen, and a screened-in breezeway connected to the garage. There was also a front porch and a smaller side porch. Upstairs was a large, dormitory-like bedroom for the six boys that included a big walk-in closet. The basement was as large as the entire house. The basement had been painted, and because it was cool, beds had been set up so the boys could sleep there on hot evenings. In fact, the basement was so big the boys used it as a place to roller-skate.

It was a much nicer house for the family—and quite grand. The side yard even had a circular, cement, two-foot-deep goldfish pond. The previous owners had had a large garden behind the house, but now it was the neighborhood football field and gathering spot. The new family in town with six handsome boys became well-known in no time. This was now the new Davis homestead, where I'd celebrate special occasions with my family for the rest of my life.

CHAPTER 24

My New Life In Sylacauga

During those early years in Sylacauga, Buddy and I were part of the Cotton Festival, a special event at Sylacauga's Recreational Center sponsored by Avondale Mills. The design department was responsible for planning the affair, and I thought the whole thing was Mr. Comer's idea to publicize the mill and promote its contribution to the community.

At the event, young men and women would wear fashionable clothes made from cotton, and a *King and Queen of Cotton* would be selected and would receive a prize. I wore the dress I'd made for Alabama College's draping class's fashion show, the formal, off-one-shoulder, blue-striped evening gown. There was a festive party with a live, local band. On this particular year, would you believe that Buddy and I were chosen?! Mr. Comer was one of the judges, and he crowned us. We tried to act dignified as we received the prize as king and queen, even though we were sitting on bales of cotton. Buddy was very embarrassed and uncomfortable with all the attention, but I thought the whole thing was hilariously fun and exciting.

Since the event was sponsored by the mill, I'm sure everyone thought the selection was rigged. Indeed, the event was nothing more than a public relations strategy. There was a full review of the event in the *Sylacauga News*, along with pictures that included me and Buddy sitting on the cotton bales.

Many years later, my family was looking at a scrapbook I'd put together. My brother-in-law saw the newspaper picture and said, "Well, there's ol' Gomer Pyle. Sho' ' nuff, there's ol' Gomer Pyle." Jim Nabors was a big television actor of the 1960s. He played the character Gomer Pyle in *The Andy Griffith Show,* a tv sitcom about life in a fictional small town called "Mayberry." His character was a popular one, and he later starred in a spinoff show called *Gomer Pyle, U.S.M.C.* He was also a wonderful singer and recorded over thirty albums. Jim Nabors was born and raised in Sylacauga, AL. Seeing his picture reminded me that he was the man who'd tapped Buddy's shoulder several times the night of that Avondale Mills event, and I'd danced with him. He called me several times afterward, asking me to go out, but I never accepted. As the new girl in town, I was often asked for dates, but I was only interested in Buddy.

For a special date, Buddy asked me to go to Birmingham to hear Tommy Dorsey and his orchestra. I suggested he ask an acquaintance, Gene Jobson, to ask Frances for a date so they could come with us. Gene owned the dry cleaning business Frances and I used to press our show wardrobes. Buddy and Gene picked us up at the boarding house, and Gene had a beautiful corsage for Frances. Frances accepted the thoughtful flowers, and before I knew what was happening, she was rushing me upstairs behind her. She took her corsage apart and made two, one for each of us. She knew how to make a corsage and wanted me to have flowers too. Buddy seemed embarrassed about it. It *was* a bit extravagant. And at the event, nobody had a corsage except us.

One weekend, the mill's chauffeur drove Frances, Ann, and me to Atlanta for fashion shows in the Magnolia Room at Rich's Department Store. After several days of shows, we were to fly back to Alabama. In the meantime, Buddy phoned me at the hotel where we were staying and said he planned to drive to Atlanta after his night superintendent shift was over, and we'd go sightseeing. The morning we were to return to Alabama, the mill chauffeur met the three of us in the hotel lobby to drive us back to Alabama, but I was waiting for Buddy.

When he arrived, we checked his map to plan our tour. We started out visiting the Fox Theatre in downtown Atlanta. Daddy told me he'd once attended an outstanding performance of opera tenor Enrico Caruso at the Fox, so I was elated to see the historical building located at the corner of Peachtree Street and Ponce de Leon Avenue for myself.

Leaving Atlanta, we drove on an unpaved, two-lane road to see the unfinished carving of three prominent confederate leaders on Stone Mountain—Jefferson Davis, Robert E. Lee, and Stonewall Jackson—which I'd studied about in art history. We went to the well-known Pittypat's Porch Restaurant for an early dinner. It was certainly more grandiose and spectacular than Maggie Bell's house in Sylacauga. We did some more sightseeing before driving back to Sylacauga that evening.

Buddy gave me a watch for Christmas that year. I wasn't expecting such a special gift. I gave him a cashmere sweater, knowing he didn't have a fashionable civilian wardrobe. I truly enjoyed spending time with him, deeply loving his kind, gentle, sweet personality. His quiet, reserved demeanor seemed a lot like my daddy's social manner. Daddy never wanted attention but was a leader at work and at home. Like my daddy, Buddy could be introverted in social situations but an analytical deep thinker and a dependable, reliable, kind person in everyday life.

I was in love with my hero, my friend.

Before that year was over, Buddy was asking me to marry him every time we got together. It was never a get-down-on-your-knee proposal but more of a discussion about the prospects of marriage. He asked me again and again. I hesitated to make such a decision so soon. It seemed so quick; I was still young, and I'd just started my dream job at the mill. I told him I'd marry him "someday." He wanted me to go ahead and set our wedding date, but I wasn't ready yet.

Eventually we made another visit to my parents' home in Tuscaloosa. It turned out he wanted to get Daddy's permission and blessing. Buddy was that kind of guy. We were at the Sunday dinner table when he asked Daddy for "Miss Peggy's" hand in marriage. Daddy calmly replied, "I think Miss Peggy is the one to make that decision. We want what she wants." (Daddy had never called me "Miss Peggy" before, and I found this amusing.) Now Buddy could check off that traditional *permission* obligation from his to-do list.

Buddy gave me a beautiful engagement ring. He said goodbye to ole Jeannie and purchased a green Nash as our honeymoon car. He also planned our honeymoon. He wanted to keep it a surprise and only gave me the most general of details.

Now the ball was in my court. I had a wedding to plan.

CHAPTER 25

Wedding Day Worries

The date was set: June 12th, 1948. I knew very little about weddings, and though I'd be winging it, I was going to give it my best effort. None of my childhood friends had married yet, except Mary Jean, and she'd eloped when I was in DC. I'd never even attended a wedding other than Jack's (my Washington, DC, coworker), and it'd been quite a formal affair.

I started planning a small garden wedding to be held on the front lawn of my family's new home in Tuscaloosa. My plan was not taken from a book; I just had a visual picture in my mind that I followed. Borrowed folding chairs would face the archway in the fence in the front yard. The reception would be through the gate in the side yard around the fishpond.

Mother put in an order for white gladiolus from her friend who had a flower farm. Her friend told us we could use all the unsold ones that would fit our plan. She also told us where we could find vines in the nearby woods for decorating the fence and pond.

Buddy's mother, Miss Laura, who was a hostess at the college's official events, loaned us her punch bowl, cups, and ladle, and shared her personal punch recipe. I ordered the cake. I didn't like the formal black-and-white outfits on the traditional cake topper, so I ordered the silver one. I didn't realize the silver ones were meant for a twenty-fifth anniversary until I had one twenty-five years later. I spray painted that same cake topper gold for our fiftieth wedding anniversary.

My choice of who would officiate our wedding was a businessman from Birmingham who'd been helping our little Montevallo church congregation. He'd never performed a wedding ceremony, but he was an amateur photographer, so I asked him to perform the ceremony and take pictures as well. I didn't want my wedding to be a big expense for my parents. I regret it now, though, as I have no good pictures of our wedding, the decorations, or any of the festivities. However, I had one studio picture that Buddy liked, and I used it for our wedding announcement.

I designed and made my wedding dress and veil—a dotted Swiss tea-length dress with a scalloped hemline and ruffles at the neckline. For my sister Faye's maid of honor dress, I made a similar garment of pink dotted Swiss. Everything was planned. I went to Tuscaloosa, ready to get started.

On the day of the wedding, Daddy and I got up around five in the morning and went to the woods to gather vines. Then we headed out to the farm to pick up the gladiolus. We ended up with six milk churns full of gladiolus, too many to count. The whole family was busy preparing for the big event. We waited until it was cooler in the afternoon to decorate with the flowers.

Using an iron rod, Daddy made holes in the ground around the fence and beside the gate, the pond, and house. I put the gladiolus stems in the holes, so it looked like they were actually growing there. I covered the arch at the gate with flowers and draped the fence with vines. We weaved gladiolus in the iron fence around the pond and put blossoms on the table around the cake and serving dishes. We floated all the leftover blossoms in the fishpond. Faye and Mother were busy getting the table ready, making sure everything was in place and overseeing the wedding preparations with help from friends. Of course, the boys were playing around as if they were helping.

While everyone was busy in the yard getting ready for the reception; placing flowers; setting out dishes, food, and cake; and getting into each other's way doing whatever had to be done, I looked up and saw the first guests from Montevallo arriving. There was my mentor, Miss Eddy, and my art instructors, Mrs. Kennedy and Mrs. Barnes. Oh, this was much too early!

There I was—hot and sweaty from helping with the decorations, dressed in old clothes with a bandana around my head to cover my pin curls. I stopped in my tracks! I was aghast and surely must've looked it too. Inside my head and body, I was screaming, *AAAAHHH!* I ran from the yard through the breezeway into the house. I was *not* ready.

Exhausted and overheated, I rushed into the cool basement to shower and put on my wedding dress. After my shower I fell on one of the beds and started crying my eyes out. I was stressed beyond my limits and totally overwhelmed. Magically, Gladys appeared.

Gladys was a family friend who'd lived with us years ago when she was in her late teens. She had been my mother's helper and helped run the household. We'd lost touch with her, but she'd read about my engagement and wedding plans in *The Birmingham News*, and here she was. She consoled me, managed to calm me down, removed the pin curls from my hair, and got me dressed. She hadn't been part of my plan at all; to this day I believe an angel must have sent her to me.

Finally, I rushed upstairs to the living room all dressed, hair fixed, tears gone, and makeup applied. But there was no Buddy or his best man, Slugger. *Where were they? It was time to start!* Mother must've murmured something about Buddy not coming and that it looked like her daughter was being left at the altar. We heard Obbie, my childhood sweetheart, say, "I'll marry her." It broke the tension, and we all laughed. The recorded songs I'd picked out were playing, and guests were being seated.

All of a sudden, here they came. Buddy and Slugger sped past the front of the house (some would say, on two wheels) and swerved around the corner, sliding into the backyard ball field where they were supposed to park. The wide-eyed guests were caught wondering if they should dive for cover. Of course, the soft, beautiful music was drowned out by their speeding car. What a dramatic, heart-pounding entrance! Certainly not the kind of thing I envisioned on my wedding day, but at this point I was just glad Buddy had made it.

There was no time to ask why Buddy and Slugger were late, but my groom was there. It was time to start. *Let the wedding begin!*

A music student from the University of Alabama sang "Ave Maria" (Mother's choice). He and his girlfriend then sang the love song "Always" (my choice). After the songs, Buddy and Slugger took their places at the picket fence archway, along with Obbie and Faye. On cue, the recording of the Wedding March began. Daddy and I walked out the front door, across the porch, and down the steps, and made our way down the aisle. I took it all in.

I saw the wedding guests dressed for the occasion in all their finery. I noted the decorations, the beautiful archway, and gladiolus everywhere. I was so happy with all our hard work. It started at 5 a.m. in the woods, then the flower farm at 6 a.m., and long into the day. It was perfect—it *was* magical. I was *so* happy as I walked toward my husband-to-be. I was the luckiest girl in the world!

Buddy and I said our vows and exchanged rings, but we didn't kiss once we'd finished. I didn't even know it was traditionally expected! We didn't have a dress rehearsal, and the businessman/first-time wedding officiant didn't tell us to, so there was no kiss. He just said, "May I present Mr. and Mrs. T. D. Woods." He extended the invitation for the reception just beyond the gate, and the guests gathered there after the ceremony.

We cut our large cake, and friends and family helped serve guests. My three youngest brothers served mints and nuts and looked so cute wearing their white shirts and white short pants. My youngest brother, Hugh, was still a small child; he passed out nuts and mints, telling guests not to take too many because we might not have enough.

Later we learned why Buddy and Slugger were late. Because of Slugger, they didn't leave the hotel in time. They had to drive down 15th Street to get to the house, and a freight train blocked the street as Buddy and Slugger were on their way. Slugger, again! I should've guessed Slugger was at fault. Buddy, my new husband, was never late.

CHAPTER 26

Our Honeymoon

As we left for our honeymoon, we came out the side door from the dining room where I threw my flower bouquet. We ran to the rental car waiting for us, decorated with "Just Married" in white shoe polish, and empty tin cans were hanging from the rear bumper. Slugger drove us over to the University of Alabama campus where Buddy had hidden his new green Nash, the honeymoon car. It was hot as blazes, and I was totally exhausted, but we were both so glad to be married and on our way.

I'd purchased everything on sale—a lovely beige suit, lizard shoes with matching bag, and a fancy straw hat—for my going away outfit. I'd been so involved with what to wear I didn't think about the fact that a heavy synthetic wool purchased at the end of a winter sale was not suitable for a June wedding outfit. The full circular skirt over two petticoats was heavy, uncomfortably hot, and totally inappropriate. I should have known better; I was, after all, a dress designer. Ha!

After we got out of Tuscaloosa, I climbed into the back seat and took off my waist pincher, petticoats, and hose. With all the car windows wide open for cool, moving air, I slept all the way to Chattanooga where Buddy had made our reservation at the Plaza Hotel. I still have the key to the room where we spent our first night together.

The next morning, we attended a church service, then were on our way to Gatlinburg, Tennessee, the next stop on our honeymoon journey. Buddy had chosen a beautiful mountain retreat in the Great Smoky Mountains, built as living quarters for Tennessee Valley Authority (TVA) workers during WWII. (His sister, May, was still living and working there.) It was a popular honeymoon destination in 1948 for returning WWII veterans.

CHAPTER 27

Back to Work at the Mill

Buddy rented a room in Sylacauga to be waiting for us when we returned from our weeklong honeymoon. He also registered his name on a list for a small, one-bedroom apartment in a duplex recently built for returning WWII veterans. A place became available to us in no time, so we made a quick weekend trip to Sears, Roebuck, and Co. in Birmingham to buy furniture. We furnished our small kitchen, living room, and bedroom for only five hundred dollars total! We had a place to stay, everything was in order, and now we could settle into our new life.

One summer, Buddy and I were chosen to go with a busload of Avondale Mills employees to the company-owned retreat on the Gulf of Mexico, near Panama City, FL. Camp Helen was one of three recreational camps owned by the company for workers' benefits. I had no idea what this trip was all about. Our new friends the Wilsons, who lived across the street from us, were also invited. Mr. Wilson was a newly graduated textile engineer, and his wife was often one of our models. They were, like us, recently married. Other mill employees were on the bus as well, but no one seemed to know what the trip was about.

We arrived at our destination and were assigned cabins similar to our honeymoon mountain cabin. What an interesting and entertaining long weekend this was going to be. Kinda like another honeymoon for the Woods and Wilsons! Everyone was curious about what was happening, but everything was finally explained when we gathered as a group.

At this first meeting, everyone from the mill was formally introduced. We were also introduced to representatives and photographers from *Look* magazine. They gave us information and directions about our roles for a pictorial magazine story yet to be written. Avondale Mills was going to be featured in an article about life for those working at the mill. Well, this was certainly news to all of us!

That evening we had a big social event—an oyster roast on the beach. An oyster roast was something I'd never even heard of. We all felt as if we were being treated like royalty. Everyone mingled and got to know each other, and it was a great evening.

The real fun began early the next morning. Representatives from *Look* staged and shot pictures of us engaging in activities they'd planned beforehand. There were competition games and group walks along the beach, and there was sailing on the Gulf of Mexico aboard the company-owned schooner. *What a life!* What an unforgettable experience.

The story in *Look* magazine wasn't published until August 1949, with a full-size headline, "THE PLANT THAT RUNS ON HAPPINESS: Bosses and Employees at Avondale Mills are Partners, and Everybody Splits the Profit." It was a feature article, as promised, complete with tons of pictures (some were full-page spreads) of employees enjoying themselves at the company retreat. I was happy to see that Buddy and I were in several of them.

The article featured a young family living in a self-owned, brick home, with both husband and wife working at the mill, as their parents had also done before them. Indeed, the article painted a happy picture of the sizable cotton textile industry that had some economic hurdles to jump through at that time. It was all about the efforts of cotton mills to stay alive economically during the invasion of synthetic fabrics and the overseas manufacturing threats of cheap labor. I realized later the purpose of the *Look* magazine article was to promote Avondale Mills with its employee incentives and portray the general importance of keeping the textile and cotton mills open and profitable.

CHAPTER 28

A Necessary Change

I loved my job in the design department at the mill. I loved designing fashions, traveling to different cities for fashion shows, and socializing with peers in the trade. At the same time, Buddy was stuck as the night superintendent at the mill.

He began looking at other job opportunities, one of which was a newly posted superintendent job at Avondale Mill's Birmingham location. He was qualified and had high hopes, but surprisingly, the job went to Slugger. It was rumored the mill workers thought Slugger wasn't qualified. Even though he was a *college Joe*—outgoing, knew how to relate to others, and made people feel at ease—Slugger knew absolutely nothing about textile engineering.

Buddy was deflated after Slugger got the position. Buddy had been looking forward to that promotion. After talking to some top staff members, I later became convinced that Buddy would've gotten the superintendent job if my own job wasn't a factor. Apparently the mill's president, Mr. Hugh Comer, didn't want anything to disrupt his new promotional department, and if Buddy left the mill, I'd be going with him.

I felt guilty thinking I might've become a handicap to Buddy's career. We discussed it and decided I should stay the course, but after that lost promotion opportunity, things weren't the same for Buddy at work. He was ready for a change—ready to start looking elsewhere.

About this time, it was spring, and I was excited to discover I was pregnant. My coworker, Frances, had married earlier that year and was expecting also. This would certainly upset the design department. I kept working and provided the commentary for our fashion show engagements during the last few months of my pregnancy. On Monday, January 30th, 1950, our little boy, Thomas Dargin Woods, III, was born. Named after his father and grandfather, we called him *Tommy*. Since Buddy had always been called by his nickname, there'd be no mistaken name-calling involved.

Buddy continued to consider better working opportunities. The night shift superintendent job was getting tiresome, and his work hours were undesirable for a family man. In the spring of 1950, he saw an ad seeking a mill superintendent at the LaFayette Cotton Mill in Lafayette, Georgia. LaFayette was a North Georgia community just south of Chattanooga, Tennessee. This small town was called the "Queen City of the Highlands," an area rich in history and natural beauty. It looked promising, so he responded to the ad and made an appointment for an interview.

In June, we drove up to the little town in the valley of Lookout Mountain. It was a majestic area, but my excitement dwindled as I noticed the town and the very small mill were nothing like Avondale Mills in Sylacauga.

While Buddy was interviewed by the local manager of the LaFayette mill, baby Tommy and I rode around town. I was disheartened by what I saw, especially the shabby mill houses in the village and the ramshackle church. I drove back to the mill and parked, feeling my anxiety growing by the minute. Then Buddy came out to the car, smiling. He excitedly told me they had offered him the superintendent job.

"What do you think?" he asked. He seemed very pleased, and it warmed my heart; I certainly didn't want to be an obstacle in all of this. Besides, I was happy enough with my baby. It was a decision for Buddy—his alone to make. He accepted their offer, and we drove back to Alabama and started making plans for the move and a new life.

I was leaving Alabama . . . again. Leaving my dream job. Eastward bound to Georgia, to the small, northwestern town of LaFayette. It was sure to be another adventure, but this time there was no feeling of excitement in my being.

CHAPTER 29

LaFayette Mills and Motherhood

With heavy hearts, we packed our bags and waved goodbye to Sylacauga, the place where I'd met and married Buddy, where I'd had my dream job, and where my son was born. There were so many memories there, and it was a bittersweet departure.

In the summer of 1950 we headed east to Georgia, then north to LaFayette. We rented a room with an adjacent small, hot kitchenette. It was a miserable, blazing mid-July, so we bought fans and endured the sweltering heat. During the cooler parts of the day, I strolled the baby outside just to get out of the house. All the while, we looked for a permanent place to live.

We found a two-bedroom apartment in a duplex on the main highway near Buddy's worksite. We gladly moved in. I was now happy and busy caring for a crawling baby boy, being a housewife, and cooking for Buddy. Thankfully he could walk home at noon for a hot meal. I tried to blend into the small-town culture, but it wasn't easy. I was an outsider, not part of the small town's tight-knit clique. In truth, I was happy in our own home and much too busy with my little family to worry about blending in.

Around Thanksgiving, I thought I might be pregnant again. I felt totally wiped out with morning sickness and had zero energy. I seriously needed help. I made an appointment to see a local family doctor in LaFayette. He confirmed I was indeed pregnant, although I'd pretty much figured that out on my own. He told me I was due in August.

We went to visit my parents in Tuscaloosa for the fall holidays. My sister, Faye, had been attending the University of Alabama but decided to take a break. I suggested she come stay with us. After Christmas, she returned to LaFayette with us, which turned out to be a real godsend for me, Buddy, and Tommy. It also was a stroke of luck for Faye. A few years earlier she'd taken elementary education courses back in Montevallo. The first spring she lived with us she was asked if she'd like to finish out the year as a substitute teacher for a small country school. What an opportunity for her! She took the job and enjoyed it, and the school asked her to return the next year as their full-time first-grade teacher.

The closest hospital to LaFayette was in Chattanooga, and even though I'd already seen a doctor, Buddy and I felt Tuscaloosa, AL, was the best place to have proper care during my delivery. I made an appointment with a Tuscaloosa obstetrician, and he moved my due date up to mid-July because the baby was so big.

The mill always closed during the week of July 4th, so Buddy took us back to Tuscaloosa to wait for the arrival of our second baby. But that wasn't happening. Buddy had to return to Georgia after the holiday shutdown, while I remained in Tuscaloosa, waiting for the baby. July passed. Still no baby. You can't imagine how hot, sticky, and unbearably humid it gets in Tuscaloosa in the summer. Seriously not a good time to be pregnant. The big attic fan was wonderfully cool at night. I missed Buddy but enjoyed being with my family during that miserable time. I certainly enjoyed Mother's good cooking, but I gained too much extra weight. I was *so* mentally and physically ready for our baby to come.

It was now Tuesday, August 14th, 1951, more than a month past my revised due date. I was driving my youngest brother,

Hubert, to the dentist. We had to cross over the rough 15th Street railroad tracks to get to the dentist's office.

Ooh—not feeling so well . . . my discomfort became obvious.

When we got home, Mother realized my stomach cramps were serious. She called Daddy to come home and take me to the emergency room. Daddy seemed very nervous and anxious, even though he and Mother had experienced eight pregnancies and hospital visits themselves. I was sensing a hidden urgency I was unfamiliar with. Daddy's driving was much faster than usual, and I became a little concerned.

Everything was vastly different with this pregnancy. During my first pregnancy, I gained very little weight and had zero morning sickness, and my mother had come to stay with me. I had a natural childbirth with the primary doctor at the mill in Sylacauga delivering Tommy. This delivery experience, though, was completely different. The Druid City Hospital in Tuscaloosa was being renovated, so I was rushed to a hospital temporarily utilizing Quonset huts that previously housed German prisoners of war during World War II. This massive, fenced-in area was about a mile from my family's home, just off 15th Street.

My doctor was busy with a patient in the Quonset hut emergency room when I arrived. When he came to my bedside, he asked if I'd be willing to take an epidural shot. I told him he was the doctor, and I was in no condition to be making serious decisions. He had me sit up, then he put the shot into my lower back. The nurse ordered me to lie back down quickly so the numbness would settle where it needed to. I wasn't familiar with that new shot, but I quickly learned I *loved* it.

The doctor appeared to be focused on his other patient, and it seemed things weren't going well for her. He spoke angrily with his nurse, using foul language and shouting orders. I told him when he came over to my side that I wished he would calm down. "This is a special, happy day in my life, and I want to remember it with joy," I said. He settled down, immediately apologized, and implied he was in an unusual situation. He was visibly frazzled but seemed to acknowledge his behavior was unprofessional and calmed down a bit.

I'd picked up on the fact that this other patient was having her baby too soon—around her seventh month—and it was a serious situation. When he came to check on me again, he'd pulled himself together and told me it was definitely time for me to deliver the baby. I couldn't believe it. He instructed me to "push hard," which I did. With that one big push, my baby came into this world without a bit of pain (nothing like the eighteen hours of hard labor that'd come with the birth of my first child). I was so very happy to be told I had a fine, big, healthy *girl*. Just what I wanted! I was quickly moved out of the ER to a private room in another Quonset hut. My doctor could now deal with his other patient who obviously needed him. Thank goodness my job was done.

After getting settled into my room, they brought in my little baby girl and put her on my tummy. I thought she was asleep, but no! She popped her little head straight up and looked at me and around the room with those big, beautiful eyes. The nurse got so excited she ran out, telling the other nurses to come see this inquisitive newborn who was lifting her head already. My little girl seemed so eager to check out her new world. Rebekah Frances Woods. My little Bekah. Now I had a son and a daughter, and I couldn't be happier.

In September of 1951 we returned to LaFayette, taking Faye with us to start her first real teaching job. In many ways this time was molding the future for my sister. She rented a room with our landlady on her side of the duplex, but Faye continued to have her meals with us. Later that year she moved with us to an eight-room house, a pink one, just outside of town. She helped me with two babies, and I helped her out in any way I could. It was a family thing.

I needed to lose baby fat, and Faye wanted to trim down a bit too. I planned and cooked the right food for us, and, sticking to our plan, we both lost weight. With Faye's weight loss, she gained tremendous confidence and got a little pep in her step. After teaching first grade in LaFayette using a provisional teaching certificate that year, she returned to Alabama to finish college in

Montevallo. During that time, she lived with our dearly beloved widowed Grandma Mahan in Clanton, Alabama. Faye served as her companion and drove Papa Mahan's Buick back and forth between Montevallo and Clanton as needed.

Faye thanked me years later for helping and encouraging her during that time in her life. I was happy to learn I'd had a role in her decision to continue her education and work with children; she found it extremely rewarding. Years later, she and her husband established a Christian elementary school. It feels good now to know I had a positive influence in her life.

LaFayette Mills was a small mill. Once Buddy began working with the company, he realized the mill was not stable; it wasn't prospering. After three years working there, he learned the mill was being bought by a foreign company. During the transition, he scouted for better employment. In his search, he learned that Lindale Mill, owned by the Pepperell Manufacturing Company in Lindale, Georgia, had an opening that sounded interesting. He applied for the job, interviewed, and was offered the position of quality control manager.

CHAPTER 30

Living in Lindale, GA

The children were still young in 1953 when we moved south of LaFayette to Lindale, also in the northwestern part of Georgia. Pepperell Manufacturing Company, a well-known New England-based company, was larger and offered more job security than the mill in LaFayette. Lindale was a suburb of Rome, approximately five miles away. I couldn't believe my luck when I discovered Rome was the home of two colleges—Berry College and Shorter College. Oh, the joy of being near a college community again!

We settled into a pleasant mill house in the supervisor's housing section of Lindale Mill. I was much happier with this town's living conditions, and a new pattern of life quickly developed. I was so relieved to have a convenient local church to attend, and there I made a new church friend who was an artist. We enrolled in an evening painting class at Shorter College. I felt happy about this opportunity to get into art again; I hadn't painted since leaving college, and I'd missed it.

My life was becoming more complete, happy, and blessed. I became a part of the community. I joined the Lindale Garden

Club, where I learned the art of flower arranging, among other horticultural activities. In addition, I became part of a group of young mothers who organized our schedules so each of us could have a weekly *free day*. We rotated who'd be in charge of a *play day* for the children, and the other moms could have a day out. This was a friendly atmosphere, and I immediately made many friends. I was completely enveloped in the pure joy of being a mother during those treasured years.

There were so many times when I was amazed by my two little ones. Often our neighbor's bird dog, Duke, stood by our backyard fence, looking over into our yard. We told Bekah not to be afraid of Duke, assuring her he was a friendly dog. We'd explain to her that bird dogs help hunters see a bird by standing very still while looking toward where the birds are. One day, Bekah was in the backyard, and there was Duke at the fence, looking at her. When she came back in the house, she said, "That bird dog thinks me a bird!"

Another time an unexpected question came from Tommy. At the supper table, he piped up, "Where did I come from?" It was much too soon for that question from our five-year-old. I didn't know what to say. All I could think of was to put the chore of answering onto someone else, so I blurted out, "Ask Poppy." Poppy replied to his young son, "You came from a seed." Tommy matter-of-factly responded, "Oh, I thought I came from LaFayette." We enjoyed those early years of their inquisitive childhoods. They were just growing up too fast. Our wonderful children completed our happy lives.

CHAPTER 31

Working Woman, Again

When Tommy started first grade and Bekah was in preschool, I had a lot of free time. I began to miss the career I had had years ago, so I considered looking for part-time work, preferably where I could use my art and fashion background. I called the largest department store in Rome, GA, and arranged an interview.

The man who interviewed me was the store manager. During the long session he asked questions about my former jobs and explained what I'd be responsible for should I be offered a position with their store. I'd be handling all the store and window displays, planning all their advertising, and regularly producing fashion shows. It sounded like a full-time public relations job. He explained that his assistant had been doing these things, but he had recently been promoted to another store location. I would be taking his place. And the salary? I was shocked! All that responsibility for a salary slightly more than that of a salesclerk. *Wow!* What he was offering wouldn't be enough to pay someone to care for the children while I worked. I couldn't help but wonder what his assistant had been paid. Then the realization hit me: he was offering such a low salary because I was a woman.

I boldly, maybe a bit angrily, asked if his assistant had worked for the same wages he was offering me. He didn't answer. He just looked at me with a red face and knew the gig was up. I stood and left, muttering some sort of opinionated statement about the absurdity of that offer under my breath. I could almost feel the steam bursting out of my ears.

Buddy's surprised reaction to my spur-of-the-moment interview brought us to a discussion about our future as a family. Buddy's life had been drastically impacted by the unexpected death of his father. Times were tough enough *before* Buddy's father died; plus, he'd been self-employed and died without a life insurance policy in place.

Buddy asked me, "What would you do if you were faced with the same situation my mother had to deal with at such a young age?" His mother had been a music major in college, and her only real marketable skills were her charming personality and her proficiency at playing the viola. She was not prepared to provide financially for her family, so she returned to her parents' home, the Lyman House, in Montevallo. Her only income there came from the college where she worked as a social hostess and from the rent from teachers who stayed in her family home.

I, on the other hand, was the oldest of eight Davis children. There was no way I could expect to return to the Davis household with my two children. Since I now had free time, Buddy and I decided it would be a good idea for me to take classes in the education department at Shorter College. This would give me a provisional certification to teach. It would be our *insurance policy.*

The eye-opening retail interview inadvertently set the stage for my future life. I was about to head back to college to prepare myself to be self-sufficient, should the need arise. Since I'd already enrolled in painting classes at Shorter, it was easy to get two elementary education classes scheduled as well. Once again, I felt the hand of providence leading me along.

CHAPTER 32

Family Visits

No matter where Buddy and I lived, as the oldest sibling and their "other mother," I always expected my young brothers to visit us during the summers. Roy came the summer of 1953 when we were in Lindale. Roy was quite handy, and I got him to help me put linoleum flooring down in our first little mill house. He spent the summer with us, playing with the kids. Buddy even taught him how to drive on our backcountry roads.

We moved from the little house into a larger one, and another brother, Paul, came to visit us. Mother was in New Orleans at the time with my sister, who was having her first child, Ray. Paul had a secret plan. He chose that specific time to elope. He got one of Roy's suits, then he and Jane, his sixteen-year-old sweetheart, drove over to Columbus, Mississippi, to get married. She'd let Paul keep the car her brother had given her, which was a big deal for an eighteen-year-old boy. Jane's brother, a piano player for gospel music's Blackwood Brothers Quartet in Memphis, TN, bought his friend Elvis Presley's pink Cadillac and gave Jane his old car. Needless to say, our family was in shock. We were shocked that

Paul had eloped, we were shocked his bride's brother knew Elvis Presley, and we were shocked her brother was now driving one of Elvis's cars.

After Paul graduated from high school in Tuscaloosa, Buddy thought he'd teach him about the importance of a college education by getting him a hard-working job in the cotton mill for the summer. Paul liked the summer job idea. He and his teen bride came to Lindale and lived with us, and our dining room became their bedroom that summer.

Paul's job at the mill was a hard, dirty one. Jane stayed with me and the children. She was like a friend, or nanny, for my and Buddy's children. They enjoyed each other. I gave Jane art lessons along with a few students I'd been asked to teach. My young sister-in-law was a good student and enjoyed painting.

That fall, when they decided to stay on in Lindale, Jane enrolled in high school, and I helped Paul register for an evening class at Shorter College. Jane's celebrity brother also bought them a trailer to live in, which they parked in the backyard of another young couple's house just outside of town.

Jane thought of me as a second mother, a counselor, someone she could talk to and learn from. At the end of the school year, she came to me in tears, terribly upset. She was five months pregnant. I was shocked I hadn't already picked up on that. She told me she'd been stopping at my house for a good breakfast every day when Tommy, Bekah, and I were at school. She confessed, too, that she'd been skipping school. I was stunned.

As she poured out her heart, she admitted she wanted to walk across the stage to accept her diploma but didn't want everyone to notice she was pregnant. She needed a white dress for the occasion. This child, as I thought of her, needed my help. I got busy making her a fashionable white dress that would conceal her pregnancy. She was very thankful and proudly walked across that stage at graduation.

One of my other brothers, John, came to visit us from Texas that summer. John was a preacher who'd graduated from Harding College. We had a small church congregation where Paul served as the song leader, and we wanted John to have a revival there. Paul and John enjoyed working together during the revival, and Buddy was baptized by John that week. It was a wonderful time, and we all hated to see John go back to Texas.

Soon after, Paul and Jane's first child, Alan, was born. The little family took the trailer and moved to Texarkana, Texas, to be near John. Paul was hired as song leader for the church where John was the minister. Paul also attended classes at a junior college and worked part time with the local newspaper. That newspaper job set the stage for Paul's life in journalism. It was a direction he followed through what became an outstanding career. He uncovered problems at Alabama's Bryce Hospital and Partlow State School and Hospital in the late 1960s and early '70s. His *Tuscaloosa News* article led to federal court decisions that set new national standards for the care of the mentally ill.

Life moved on for Paul in so many interesting ways after that. Fifty years after he started at the newspaper, he was nominated for the Pulitzer Prize in journalism. My brother had graduated from the "College of Hard Knocks" and exceeded everyone's expectations. We were so proud of him.

CHAPTER 33

Textiles and Teaching: Trion, GA

Our life was good in Lindale. We even bought property and began plans to build a house on the land. While doing so, we were surprised to learn that the mill was having an outside industrial operations study done. Buddy said this meant there were production and economic concerns at the mill. The research study report suggested that jobs which were not directly a part of production be eliminated. Unfortunately, Buddy's job in quality control was one of those.

I'm sure Buddy saw this coming, but he never said anything to me. Eventually, however, he had to let me know he no longer had a job at the mill. Thankfully the company allowed Buddy to continue working as he searched for a new job. I was embarrassed by the situation, and I didn't want to have to answer questions from friends and neighbors. I wanted to get away from curious people, think about the future, and figure out what we were going to do.

I talked to Buddy about me taking the children to visit my sister, Faye. He agreed, so the children and I took the train to New Orleans.

Buddy found a new position at Riegel Textile Mills in Trion, another cotton mill in North Georgia, close to Lindale. In the meantime, though, he was becoming more and more concerned about the value of his textile engineering degree from Clemson. He still had his GI Bill opportunity for more education as a military veteran, and he was entertaining thoughts of going into another field of work.

In 1957, we left Lindale and moved to Trion, our third move since leaving Alabama, and Buddy started his job at Riegel Textile Mills. During the early 1900s, the mills belonged to the Trion Manufacturing Company but were in decline. Over the years, the mills became plagued with anti-union conflicts, a fire, and closings. In the 1940s, the mills became the Riegel Textile Corporation when Benjamin D. Riegel, a New York businessman, purchased them. Trion became known for making denim and was called the *denim capital of the world.*

We were anxious to settle in that historic cotton mill village. We moved temporarily into a large, wooden, two-story building known as The Plaza. The Plaza had been built in the 1800s for single female mill workers but was now an antiquated hotel. We placed our meager collection of furniture in a storage unit until we could find a permanent place to live.

Soon, an eight-room house in the middle of town became available. This house was conveniently located near everything we needed. Within walking distance were two schools, as well as the Mill Hospital, the Community Recreation Center with an indoor pool, Park Avenue (the main street), the Company Store, a bank, and a general merchandise and grocery store. Eventually we ended up purchasing that house for five thousand dollars.

Our new house had a long hallway down the middle, four bedrooms, a kitchen, a living room, a dining room, two bathrooms, and a screened-in sleeping porch at one end of the front porch. In the back of the house was a garage. A room on one side of the garage included a stove and a toilet; I figured it might've served as a maid's living quarters for a time. As soon as I saw the little room, I wanted it for my art studio. I couldn't believe my good luck! For Buddy (whom we now called "Poppy" or "Pop"), there was a utility building he could use as a workshop. It was a perfect little slice of

Americana and even had a classic white picket fence around the backyard buildings. I loved it.

I eagerly dove right in making this house a home. I chose some beautiful fabrics and got busy sewing curtains and draperies. The children were happy, already making friends in school, and it seemed as if it'd be such a good place to raise them. Trion was a friendly, happening town. The children enjoyed it.

We settled into our home in the spring of 1958. Not long after, there was a knock at our door. I was surprised when I opened it and saw the local elementary school principal. My neighbor was one of their seventh-grade teachers, and she was having surgery soon and needed time off to recover. The principal was in desperate need of a replacement, and my neighbor mentioned that I was qualified to teach. So the principal walked over from the school to ask if I'd be willing to finish out the year as a substitute teacher.

This opportunity came soon after we had made the decision for me to take education courses at Shorter College. I felt blessed that God was in control of my life, and all I needed to do was follow where He led. After Pop and I considered the opportunity, I accepted the school principal's job offer. I'd finish out the last few months of school, teaching history to seventh graders. *Seventh graders? What have I done?*

It was like herding cats. I was thoroughly frustrated by the rowdy behavior of those adolescent seventh-grade boys. I complained to another seventh-grade teacher about my students' lack of interest in history, their lack of respect for me, and their overall ill-mannered attitude. She told me I needed to get tough, then laughed, saying, "I once told a boy I'd pull his arm off and hit him with the bloody nub." Wow! I was shocked and caught completely off guard by this remark, especially coming from a teacher. How could anyone say such a thing?

The next year, the elementary school needed a teacher for the third grade, and I was asked to teach full time. The thought of full-time work needed some time to sink in; to me, it was essentially the same as being drafted into the military. There was a slight sense of obligation, but more importantly I knew there was a real need. I'm a helper by nature, and I instinctively felt the urge to help whenever a particular situation arose. After Buddy and I considered the benefits this job could have for our family, I accepted the offer. I was happily following this path that appeared before me. I loved teaching (especially younger children), and with the opportunity of full-time work, this could become my new profession. I decided to go all in.

It took no time at all with those precious young third graders for me to realize that this was where I was born to be. I could certainly see myself doing it for the rest of my career. As the oldest child, I'd always helped Mother look after my younger brothers. My mother loved our big family, and I'd learned about the discipline needed to work with children from her. Now I had the freedom to share myself with these third graders, teaching them in the way I'd been taught. It was a labor of love.

The University of Georgia was offering evening extension courses at the school where I was teaching, and I wanted to enroll in classes I needed for my elementary education teaching certificate. Problem was, the University of Georgia didn't offer extension classes during the summer. So I decided to take my children with me to Tuscaloosa and stay with my parents. I took classes at the University of Alabama, and my children enrolled in the University's summer program.

It was a whirlwind few months, but after the summer session we headed back to Georgia. My children were happy to be back home where the whole community was their playground, and we were all happy to be back home with Pop. It was now 1959, and I looked forward to my second year of full-time teaching. I loved my teaching job; I felt I was contributing to the students at school and to my family at home. I was very content. We all were.

CHAPTER 34

Art In My Veins

B ack in Trion, I tried to spend time in my little art studio, cultivating my art technique. It was my special *time for me* place. I was taking an evening course at Shorter College, and my associate professor there did his thesis on earth (clay) pigment. I was eager to learn about this unusual medium and couldn't wait to paint and experiment with it. I'd already started a collection of my own pigments. My main focus was getting the house in order, so reluctantly I stowed away my art supplies in my new little studio. While the painters were busy painting the house, I went to work finishing the curtains and drapes, refinishing furniture, and adding final decorating touches. It was a busy time.

One of the items stored in my art studio was a binder for the earth pigment (it was used to hold the powdered dirt together). While stored in the studio, my gum Arabic binder (a binder medium to make watercolor paints) soured, releasing a very distinct, pungent odor. The painters wanted to know what we were "brewing" in that little room.

"It smells like white lightnin' out there," one of them said.

"No, no," I quickly assured them. "There's no white lightnin' here!"

It turned out I didn't paint much with the earth pigment; I just played around with it for fun. But I painted oil portraits of Tommy and Bekah and was commissioned to do portraits of two of their friends. I also painted a few other nice paintings. I even taught private drawing classes for children and friends. That little studio was fast becoming my cherished happy place.

The Plum Nelly Clothesline Art Show was a very popular, two-day, outdoor seasonal event in the Southern Appalachian Mountains around Chattanooga and Lookout Mountain. It was open to residents in the North Georgia region, so I contacted the show's sponsor, Fannie Mennen, regarding my paintings. Fannie was a Chattanooga art teacher who sponsored the show on her cabin property on the backside of Lookout Mountain. We set up a time for me to visit her there to discuss the possibility of showing my artwork. I packed a collection of paintings in our little Volkswagen and drove up to the area near Trenton, Georgia. She looked at my paintings, and we chatted about my background.

Fannie was very pleasant and offered me the opportunity to participate in the upcoming October show. I asked her about the show's name, and she told me the cabin had been given to her by her brother-in-law. He'd called the cabin and its property "Plum Nelly" because it was "*plum* out of Tennessee and *nearly* out of Georgia." With his southern accent, the word *nearly* sounded like *nelly*. It was the largest art event in the area, and around twelve thousand people attended the first year I had an exhibit in that show.

I participated in the show during the last few years we lived in Trion. That experience was inspirational to me, as people actually bought my paintings. I began to fully appreciate my love of art. I found it very relaxing and very peaceful, and this played a big part in my overall contentment. It gave me a beautiful outlet to express my emotions. I enjoyed it, and I felt validated in the art community, which did wonders for my self-esteem. It was a happy time.

CHAPTER 35

The Educator

Buddy was responsible for quality control at the Riegel Textile Mills in Trion, Georgia. In the 1950s, synthetic materials were taking over, and the cotton mills in the US were cutting back. Buddy saw the writing on the wall when the company paid for a production study, and he started to think of other employment options. He saw an ad and applied for a job with Georgia Duck and Cordage Mill, a smaller mill in a suburb of Atlanta called Avondale Estates. He was offered the job right after his interview, and he accepted. I stayed in Trion to finish my teaching contract while Buddy started work at his new job. He made the seventy-five-mile trip back and forth on the weekends.

Early one Monday morning, I rode into Atlanta with Buddy. He went to work, and I drove to the administrative offices of the DeKalb County School District. When I walked in, I was surprised to see no one there. I wondered where everyone was. Eventually a man walked in and I asked, "Where is everyone?" He haughtily replied, "I'm Jim Cherry, superintendent of the DeKalb County

Schools. But staff won't come in until 8:00." I hadn't realized how early I was, but I'd always heard "the early bird gets the worm"!

Sure enough, employees began wandering in, and in no time, I'd signed a contract to teach in one of the fastest-growing county school systems in the country. I was bowled over by the fact they'd hired me so quickly and could only assume they truly needed teachers to fill positions. We started looking for a house and found one we liked nearby in the little town of Stone Mountain. It was an eventful time, for sure. In 1963, as soon as school was out for the summer in Trion, we pulled up stakes once again and started another new chapter in our lives.

There came a change in the air in the 1960s, and the culture shifted dramatically, though some areas were slower to adjust. Even though it was one of the fastest-growing school systems nationwide, Mr. Cherry still had some outdated ideas. The first day I reported to school there was a mandatory meeting for all the teachers in DeKalb County. At this meeting, Mr. Cherry expressed his pride in finally getting *male* principals in *every* school in DeKalb County—twenty-two high schools and sixty-plus elementary schools. Many returning war veterans were using their GI benefits to get degrees in education, vying with the women who had taken over this responsibility during the war. However, Mr. Cherry's idea of male dominance in education was coming to an end. Within a decade, most of those positions were filled by women.

I began teaching third grade, the same grade I'd taught in Trion, and I had a good first year in this new school. However, the following year I taught the second-grade enrichment class. Enrichment classes were a new, progressive way of addressing education. These classes focused on *experiences* rather than rote memorization. The other teachers didn't want to lead the enrichment class, and I was more than happy to hear that.

I loved this way of teaching. I had as much fun as they did! I loved the freedom of being able to choose those enriching experiences as I saw fit. We visited the Atlanta airport, took a train ride to a granite quarry, churned milk to make butter, and made wax candles. We created a class newspaper, wrote an original play (making our own props), and performed our Thanksgiving drama in the auditorium for the whole school. We even wrote letters to the legendary Helen Keller and were ecstatic when she wrote back to the students. I also contacted local residents to visit our class to talk about their jobs and interests. Mr. Gems, the "rock man," was a favorite. Other visiting participants included a *New York Times* reporter (a student's father) and the manager of a local automobile dealership.

Each student was responsible for writing a thank-you letter to our visitors. One of the students wrote the dealership manager and stated her father had purchased a car from him, and it was a "lemon." She drew a picture of the car, sitting in the carport and looking sad, and included it with her letter. Honest child—she was being truthful!

One day soon after, I was called to the school office. When I got there, the principal told me there was a phone call from the manager of the car dealership, who was saying something about receiving letters from my class. The principal didn't know about the letters, didn't know what to say, and wanted me to take the call. The dealership's manager thanked me for the letters and said he shared them with his staff, especially the letter about the "lemon." During our conversation, he asked for the phone number of the father who'd purchased that unlucky car. I was pleased to find out later that the "lemon" had been replaced because of the little girl's letter and creative picture.

I soon discovered how the school district's administrative policies were affected by each individual school's politics. My enrichment classes had forty students, which was ten more than allowed, according to school policy. I learned that parents were clamoring for their children to be placed in the enrichment classes, and administrative regulations pertaining to the student-teacher ratio were not being followed. I even had students in my classroom who were listed on other teachers' classroom rolls. One child I taught began living with her aunt (in our school district) so she could attend an enrichment class.

I felt the dishonesty of this situation, and it was unsettling, but I thoroughly enjoyed my students and our experiences. We were having fun learning together, and I enjoyed creating a challenge for my students and watching them apply what they'd learned. My two coworkers jokingly said I was making it hard on myself by doing extra stuff. They didn't realize how much satisfaction I got teaching those children. I taught both enrichment and regular classes in a self-contained classroom for the next ten years, and it was just delightful.

CHAPTER 36

Art and Music

Most music classes in DeKalb County schools were taught by a music teacher, but there were no art teachers. I was asked to move from teaching a regular class to teaching art, exclusively. I wasn't sure I'd enjoy that, but I tried it for the summer, and then decided to go for it. However, teaching art would mean I needed to go back to college for a certification in art education. I knew the University of Georgia offered the courses I needed, so I began working on a master's in art education and received my degree in 1970.

Teaching art classes meant traveling to two schools, and I didn't like that idea. Because of my music background, I proposed to the administration that I remain at Avondale Elementary as an art *and* music teacher, and they agreed.

Besides teaching art and music, I was also expected to produce regular Parent-Teacher Association (PTA) music programs to motivate parent attendance. My Christmas program became a tradition. It was very rewarding but labor intensive. It meant each student from each class participated in some aspect of the show.

Since I was teaching an art class, I expected the school to provide art supplies; however, having art classes in the elementary school was new, and no one was assigned the responsibility of ordering supplies. I found a large storage room where I could keep my own supplies, and I began collecting. Eventually it was full of stuff: roadside garbage, newspapers, magazines, wire, pinecones, acorns, cardboard, bottles, ordinary junk, basically anything that could be used to create art. Buddy brought me all kinds of mill spools, yarn, machine parts, fabric, anything discarded from the mill. The school kids and I did a lot of yarn crafts, macramé, and weaving with those goodies. Buddy had some old throw-away loom bobbins that I used as rhythm sticks in music class as well. Our makeshift stash of supplies led to some very interesting, fun projects.

During those years, I regularly had student teachers, usually two or three per semester. When I believed my student teachers were ready to plan and conduct a class alone, I'd disappear into my storage room to let them try out their teaching wings. I was often proud of their progress in the real world of the art class, but as I continued to have student teachers, it became apparent that some weren't prepared to teach. There was no real lab school for the student teachers, and it was up to me to mentor them—on-the-job training, so to speak. The art classes for children were a new, innovative project, and even though the teaching students may have had art degrees, they didn't know how to teach young children.

One young lady stated she really didn't like the younger students and thought she'd enjoy teaching older ones more. Her supervisor assured her that would not be the case. He told her if she didn't like thirty little seven-year-olds, she certainly wouldn't find older adolescents easy to love . . . or even like. I figured that this young lady didn't need to be a teacher at all. I'm sure teaching children wasn't her ultimate goal when she earned her art degree.

CHAPTER 37

A Time of Transition

After several years of this heavy schedule, my friend Sarah (the DeKalb County art supervisor) told me that a position for a new elementary school art supervisor would become available next year in the county office. Sarah was technically in charge of the county high schools, but she oversaw all the art classes. She could use some help, she said, and encouraged me to apply for the position.

Sarah went to the man who was over all the elementary staff, as he'd give the final approval. She told him I was the only one with the required qualifications, as I had an art background as well as a master's in art education. According to others, he became furious, followed her on her heels out of the office, and retorted, "No dang woman's going to tell me who I can and can't hire!" Apparently he made quite a spectacle of himself, and his performance created a lot of controversy in the county office.

On the first day of school, I was in the front office signing in when an acquaintance from the county office greeted me and said, "We all thought the art job was yours. Who is this character who got it?" It quickly became apparent to everyone there that I hadn't been told the news yet. And, to add insult to injury, I later learned that a childhood acquaintance from Montevallo was the new hire. I knew she had no visual arts skills or training, nor was she certified to teach art. As I recall, she was more into drama. Oh well. . . .

That same day, the school's secretary handed me a piece of paper with a phone number on it, urging me to call it soon. I called on the spot. I didn't know at the time, but I'd been recommended to work with a new team setting up a statewide research project through the University of Georgia. I went to an interview that afternoon and was hired to be one of eight data collectors in a newly established research and development project. It seemed one door closed, and God opened a new one. Another path laid out before me, as if it was meant to be. I would be leaving the classroom as a teacher and entering the realm of educational observation and evaluation as a data collector. The timing was providential.

My initial disappointment in missing out on the art supervisor job was short lived. Furthermore, I was awfully glad to have a little step up in salary for a ten-month job instead of the typical nine-month teacher's salary. I truly felt I had an angel on my shoulder, directing me toward important opportunities where my judgment was valued and my ideas were welcomed. Plus, I got more money!

Between 1973 and 1987, I broadened my perspective and learned valuable lessons about research in the field of education. When I left, I was honored with a very nice going-away party and a plaque for having the most tenure of anyone there, as I was an original member.

When I left the research project, I started working with the DeKalb County School District's Adopt-A-School program. The program was intended to recruit volunteers from businesses to be active within the school system. I served as a liaison between the school and volunteers and planned Adopt-A-School events. After staying with the program for three years, I was ready to retire. In 1989, DeKalb County was offering a nice retirement incentive to employees. The area superintendent's office put on a lovely farewell reception for me.

Buddy needed me, and I needed to slow down and enjoy another kind of life with new daily purposes. I had another life out there waiting for me during my retirement years.

CHAPTER 38

When Life Goes Topsy-Turvy

I've lived my life with a hunger for the satisfaction I feel when I'm being helpful; I want to be needed. I suppose being the eldest in a big family has something to do with it. I thrive on the sense of purpose I feel when I've fulfilled my responsibilities or met someone's need.

This driving challenge came strongly in the 1990s when Buddy began to have minor daily needs. He turned eighty on May 4th, 1998, and that June our family honored us for our fiftieth wedding anniversary. He was so happy he'd lived that long. For years he repeatedly said he was living on borrowed time because his father had died at age fifty-one.

I started driving for us and provided stability when Buddy's equilibrium was off-kilter. "You are my walking cane," he'd say, keeping his hand on my shoulder. I placed the ornate brass bell I used when teaching school on the table next to his chair. When he needed help, he'd tap the bell, and I'd be there.

He just wanted my presence, so I stayed with him and helped him feel safe and secure. His self-diagnosis was simple: "I'm just winding down; I'm not sick," he'd say, explaining that those were his serendipity years. He never expected to reach age eighty, and I was glad to hear this man of few words tell me I was the best thing that ever happened to him.

In September, three months after celebrating fifty years of marriage, Buddy got up from his chair to get a snack without tapping the little school bell for me. He fell backward and hit his head, which resulted in a very serious concussion. On September 5th, 1998, my loving husband died as a result of that fall. He was a very kind and gentle man with an honorable character whom I loved deeply, highly admired, and greatly respected. He was a genuinely good, loving person. We had a wonderful life together. We never had arguments or angry words. He told me my wish was his command, and I felt the same way about his wishes. After his death, the beautiful fall season of colors consoled me, as it reminded me to be thankful for those happy years we had shared. But dreary days came with the falling leaves too. The dark days grew long and sad in the days that followed his passing.

By choice, I'd never involved myself in any way with our family's financial matters. After Buddy's death, it became apparent I had a lot to learn. I remembered I needed some documents from our safe-deposit box at the bank. When I opened it, I found an article Buddy had placed there for me to find. It was instructions for widows and widowers. He'd highlighted decisions a person should not make immediately after the death of a partner, suggesting a wait time of two years before making major changes. In his usual helpful, loving manner, he was still taking care of my needs even after he was gone.

I decided to register for a senior enrichment course about financial planning at a Baptist church nearby. I also purchased the book *Financial Planning for Dummies*. The course gave me a better understanding of how to handle my finances. I received a free second course and chose the woodcarving class. It provided a challenging, creative time for me to clear my mind. I had woodcarving tools I'd given to Buddy after his retirement, which he'd never used, so I used them to whittle a little dog.

My brother Willard was a bank manager in Tuscaloosa, so I asked him for advice. He said I should find a trustworthy financial planner to help me. This was the last conversation I had with Willard. He died during open-heart surgery on October 8th, 1998, a month after Buddy's death.

There was so much sadness and heartache, but I stopped and tried to look for God's blessings. My prayers were answered, and I found a wonderful financial planner, Pat King, at church. She became my good friend and gave me the financial advice and confidence I needed to carry on. We took several cruises together, which were a restful kind of help for my changing life during those times of adjustment.

CHAPTER 39

Caregiving

The loss of my life partner started a chain reaction of challenging situations. How thoughtful that just three months after Buddy's death, my brother Paul, who was living in Auburn, Alabama, reached out to me. I'd been alone for the first time in my life. Paul invited me to take a trip with him and his second wife, Gayle, to visit and check on our preacher brother, John. John was living in Beaumont, Texas, and he was going through an emotional and traumatic life situation as well.

John's beautiful wife, Gena, had been disabled for six or seven years with amyotrophic lateral sclerosis (ALS), known as Lou Gehrig's disease. John had called me recently for a big-sister chat about the frightening emergency he'd experienced on Christmas Eve. Gena stopped breathing, and he had revived her. I was deeply concerned about his situation. He was dealing with physical stress and mental anxiety, and he was facing an indefinite future. He needed his caring family, so Paul, Gayle, and I drove to Texas to spread some of that TLC over John.

We had a typical holiday visit, staying at John's home in Beaumont. After welcoming in the New Year, Paul and Gayle were ready to return home, but I simply couldn't leave my brother, who I feared was near exhaustion or mental collapse. I settled into the guest room to help him deal with the slowly declining life of his wife for however long he needed me. John told his friends he was helping me deal with the recent sudden and unexpected loss of my husband. I realized we were actually helping each other cope with our own personal situations. It was a bonding family thing for us to be together to share our family love.

I often thought, *How can I be helpful? What needs to be done?* Before I arrived, women from the church where John preached had scheduled around-the-clock visits with Gena. They were her social outlet to keep her involved in the outside world. For several years she was never left alone. It'd been a blessing to have those ladies help in that special, caring way. One of her teacher friends even helped Gena by writing a little book of Gena's sorrowful laments.

However, once I arrived and started helping, the women from the church chose not to continue their visits. Gena began to miss the cycle of friendly companions, as she soon realized my focus was not the same as the chatty social callers. I was frantically busy trying to accomplish things I felt were more helpful than just sitting with her, but that's probably not what she wanted nor needed most.

I needed to be *actively* involved. I tried to help John with the ongoing needs of the future. I got rid of boxes—big boxes full of "get well" and "thinking of you" cards—old magazines, and clothes and shoes Gena would never wear again. I was too emotionally involved to passively spend time chatting with her. I just tried to be a good listener to her sorrowful thoughts about that awful, debilitating disease. It was a sad time for everyone. Gena was in an impossible situation, John was mourning their future, and I was mourning the loss of Buddy. It'd only been a few months since he'd passed.

Unlike some ALS patients, Gena could still eat and talk as well as express her emotions and feelings. Her words, at times, tore at my heartstrings. "I am down inside my body somewhere. I just can't find myself," she said during one of those listening sessions.

She also told me she wanted to die and asked me if I thought it was a sinful desire.

I wrote Isaiah 41:10 and 13 on a large card, big enough for her to see and read, and placed it at her eye level on a bookshelf beside her bed:

> *Do not fear, for I am with you, do not be dismayed, for I am your God. I will strengthen you and help you; I will uphold you with my righteous right hand. . . . For I am the Lord, your God, who takes hold of your right hand and says to you, Do not fear, I will help you.*

Gena thanked me many times for the peace and comfort she felt as she read the verses daily. I felt a calming peace, knowing I'd helped her in a spiritual way as well as tending to her physical needs. I thought my dear brother needed my help and support as much as she did. It was a very trying situation, and I leaned on my faith heavily for comfort. I sympathized with Gena, but I couldn't imagine being in her shoes. Poor John was at his wits' end, and we were all exhausted beyond belief.

On February 13th, 1999, Gena told me to be sure to remind John to bring her his usual box of Valentine's chocolates. I didn't need to remind him. He came home that evening with a box of Hershey's chocolates. She enjoyed her chocolate treat as she closed out her day.

Gena died peacefully in her sleep that night before Valentine's Day. The night nurse ran to my bed and told me Gena had stopped breathing. I had to go tell John. Of course, this was one of the hardest things I'd ever had to do.

Since that time, John referred to me as his rescue angel. He needed me, and I finally realized I needed him too. I came back home with new thoughts as I tried to recognize and analyze the changes and challenging hills I was going to have to start climbing on my own. I was glad I had shed some light in the darkness of my brother's world, but I began to realize I had to face the uncertainties of my own life now that I was alone.

Sitting in my too-big, empty house in Stone Mountain, I pondered my next steps. The house was truly too large for me, and it no longer felt like home. I'd been thinking about Buddy's advice about not making drastic changes for two years after a life change, and now that time had come.

CHAPTER 40

My Retirement Bungalow

Getting out of that big, lonely house was number one on my challenging to-do list. I thought of the discussions Buddy and I had had years before about the potential of our rental bungalow in downtown Decatur. We had purchased the little four-room house as an investment back in 1977. At that time, I'd learned from a friend that a charming one-hundred-year-old bungalow in her neighborhood would be coming up for sale. It was in the city of Decatur, a charming little city outside of Atlanta, GA. The house sat on a pretty lot and had great restoration potential.

I thought we could afford that little house, and Buddy agreed it'd indeed be a good investment. However, he wanted me to purchase the house so it would be in my name. Doing so would help me establish my personal credit, which seemed like a wise decision. It was like a gift and an opportunity out of the blue. He explained this would mean a lot to me later. He'd learned that research predicted I'd live fourteen years longer than he would. This was typical of Buddy, and I always appreciated how he looked out for me, even my future. His unending concern always tugged on my heartstrings.

The homeowner called when the house became available, and I told him I wanted to buy it. Luckily, a church friend of mine was the CEO of Decatur Federal Savings and Loan. Another God thing. I was convinced I had an angel on my shoulder, and God had me in His hands.

I had no problem borrowing money to purchase the house. We paid fourteen thousand dollars for the charming, classic-style bungalow. I found the original *Deed of Sale* inside the house, which said it'd been sold to its first owners in 1925, the same year I was born. I think it was originally a servant's house built behind the big owners' house along Ponce De Leon Avenue, a well-known historic street ever since the Civil War.

Our little house was rented immediately and always remained rented. Buddy took care of the rental management, and it was paid off in a very short time. Our daughter, Bekah, lived there with her new little family for a while. I remember Buddy telling me in the early 1990s that our Decatur bungalow's worth was at least two hundred thousand dollars—certainly as much or more than our Stone Mountain family ranch, which had seven rooms, two bathrooms, and a daylight basement. We'd even added a huge "narnie" room to the Stone Mountain house. I called my first granddaughter "darling," but she repeated it back as "narnie," and it stuck. That special narnie room was where we held all our parties as our family grew bigger, and it was my favorite of all the rooms.

That little bungalow was worth more only because of its downtown Decatur location, but I loved the idea of living in that quaint, antique house. I started thinking creatively about how I could renovate that charming, tiny, four-room house for my new home. I started drawing my floor plan. I found a contractor who had a blueprint made based on my rough draft, and the process got started in 2000. It was exciting and stimulating to learn so much about renovation during those months, as approximately twelve hundred square feet of living space was added to the structure. After the contractor started working on it, though, he informed me the contract did not include any work on the original part of the house. So I put on gloves, parked myself on a stepladder, and worked just as hard as his construction workers, removing wallpaper, painting, and cleaning those four old rooms.

I moved into my new dwelling in early May of 2001, as the welcoming, dark-pink Japanese maple tree was in full bloom just outside my new kitchen window. How wonderful it was to have my four strong, young grandsons help make that big move a day to remember. After thirty years, I was leaving our family home. Almost miraculously, the Stone Mountain house sold the same week! I now had two big life changes checked off my new bucket list.

CHAPTER 41

Mother and Me

During the late 1980s, I made trips to check on my ninety-year-old mother living alone in Tuscaloosa in the large family home. My brother Willard died in 1988, and after that, I made more frequent trips to check on Mother. Willard ate lunch with her every day, since his bank was located just down the street from her. He enjoyed her hot meals, even though he joked about her being a very "creative, conservative cook," using all kinds of unknown leftovers in her lunch concoctions. She enjoyed talking to him about politics, children, and life in general. It was entertaining for her, getting to know him as a grown man.

Their arrangement was good for them. Willard was her caregiver in many ways, keeping her happy and content. He also gave her a feeling of security. Once when I was there, she inadvertently referred to Willard as "Daddy." She always thought of Daddy when she saw Willard coming through her breezeway wearing a hat like Daddy wore. It might've even been Daddy's old hat.

She'd been living alone since Daddy died, but now Mother was beginning to need more help, and Willard was no longer there.

I automatically felt responsible for her care. Mother had asked me to come live with her in Tuscaloosa after Buddy died, so I knew she'd been thinking about her future. Sometime in 2001, I received an urgent call from one of her church friends and again traveled to Tuscaloosa to check on her.

I asked Mother what she thought about the independent living facility her friend had reserved for her in the retirement complex she managed. Mother had never mentioned to me that her friend had approached her about moving into the retirement community. In fact, she wouldn't even check out the residence. She became very defensive when I mentioned it.

I didn't want her to think I was trying to push any solution on her. I knew she was a self-sufficient and determined person. I told her we all just wanted to know what she wanted to do because she wasn't taking care of her personal needs. She looked at me and said in a rather submissive and uncharacteristic manner, "I want to come live with you." I replied, "Well, that's what you will do." I'd been working on the restoration of the little bungalow to be my retirement home. I was now seventy-six and had known for a long time that Mother might be with me someday. Now, that time had come.

I'd been in my new little bungalow for about a year when Mother came to stay with me. We locked up her house in Tuscaloosa, packed my car, and returned to Atlanta. I parked in my two-car garage at the back of my new home and helped Mother up the eight steps. I opened the door into the little keeping room. She stepped in then fell flat on the floor! I was so very frightened and horrified by her dangerous fall, but she just laid there laughing and made a joke about it, saying, "I was so excited to see your new home, I just sprawled through the door."

That started my new, fun-time relationship with my ninety-six-year-old mother. It was a new lifestyle adjustment for me, but I think it might've been even harder for her. I had to set up some necessary rules and expectations. I thought it best to tell her, "Now, I have to be the one making most of the decisions that are best for me *and* for you." We had to discuss our new living arrangement. She had to give me the reins for this new ride. I didn't want to be treated like her child, as I'd now be the only person taking care of her needs.

The first thing I did right away was take Mother to my primary doctor, which was such a blessing for both of us. My family doctor had been a student of mine throughout her elementary school years in DeKalb County. After graduate school, she specialized in geriatric care at Emory University Hospital. She took wonderful care of Mother for the rest of her life.

We had many unusual things happen during our shared living arrangement. Mother made jokes of all of her needs, which was likely her way of coping as she got older. She attended the ladies Bible class I taught on Wednesday mornings and enjoyed getting acquainted with a new church family. One rainy morning, I parked under the church building's portico for our convenience. When we were ready to leave, I opened the passenger door to help her get inside the car. Other folks leaving the building were standing near us chatting, and they caught Mother's attention. She waved to them, lost her balance, and fell backward, knocking me down too, which cushioned her fall. The ladies came rushing over to pick her up while she cracked a joke about it. Finally, I said to my friends, "Hey, I'm down here too! Can I get a bit of help?"

Many times, Mother slipped out of her lift chair into a sitting position on the floor. She laughed at my efforts as I struggled to get her up off the floor. One night, she fell out of bed, and I had to call 911 because I couldn't pick her up. Eventually I purchased a hospital bed with a side rail, got her a wheelchair, renovated her bathroom to make it wheelchair accessible, and added a ramp to the front porch. Not only did I make structural changes to the house, but I also changed my daily routine to meet her needs.

Mother was very independent but did give me control of our daily lives. Still, I wanted to hear from her that I was doing a good job, or at least that she appreciated my efforts. A friend of mine visited and asked her directly, "Is Peggy taking good care of you?" Mother answered, "She should; I took care of her." Later I had a conversation with Mother and explained that my motivation for helping her was not based on a need to pay back debts; it was based on love.

A long time after our discussion about expressing appreciation and gratitude, Mother responded verbally as I tucked her into bed one night. I gave her a goodnight kiss and told her I loved her, and she shouted out to me as I was leaving her bedroom, "I love you too, and I appreciate everything you've ever done for me." This was so out of character for her, and it surprised me. I think an angel told her to say that because I really and truly needed to hear it. I was so touched my eyes teared up, and I will forever cherish that moment.

In September of 2009, I called the doctor around 4 p.m. and told her I'd noticed Mother's legs were swollen, and she was breathing about eight times to my one. She told me to bring her into the office immediately, and she'd wait for us to arrive. She examined Mother in the office and sent us to the emergency room. Mother was diagnosed with congestive heart failure and admitted to the hospital. She was very sick, but I figured she'd be going home in a few days.

My brother Hubert came to sit with her to give me a break. It was then that he informed me they were packing her up to move. This was how I found out Mother needed to go to hospice. I was absolutely devastated. As sad as I was, though, I was determined to make this transition as easy as possible for her. I brought pictures for her bedside table and a familiar oil painting to hang on the wall so she might feel more at home. I informed family and friends of the situation, and everyone offered support and prayers.

Family and church friends stopped by to visit Mother for the few days she was in hospice. One night I stayed past midnight, sitting with her and talking to her, assuming she was hearing me, although she hadn't spoken all day. As I started to leave, I told her I was going on to bed and hoped she'd have a good, restful night. It was raining outside, and as I was putting on my raincoat, she opened her eyes for the first time that day and literally shouted out to me, "I'm doing just fine." (My mother was nearly deaf.) As I drove home in tears in the pouring rain, I could still hear her shouting, "I'm doing just fine." I felt like the angels were crying with me. I'm certain they gave her those last words to say just for me.

I had just gotten to sleep at about two in the morning when Hugh called me. Hospice had called him to say our mother had died, and they couldn't get me on the phone. I immediately got dressed and returned to the hospice house, thinking she probably passed on just as I left her bedside. I'm so thankful for her last words. She had a peaceful end. She was 104 years old.

I'd previously made the arrangements for my mother's burial in Clanton, Alabama, where we had a graveside service. Tuscaloosa friends came on a bus for her service in Clanton, and then, two days later, on September 26th, 2009, we had a memorial service back in Georgia at my church, Northlake Church of Christ.

Mother and I had eight fun and challenging years together. I have no regrets about the care I gave her, as I feel I did my best. She had a good husband—never a cross word between them—and a good life raising eight good children who loved and respected her. I miss her to this day.

CHAPTER 42

Oh-So-Secret Secrets

I'll always have memories from the jobs I had in my life: the OSS, my five-year dream job in the fashion industry, and my thirty-one years as an educator. Some of the most blessed years of my life, though, were as a stay-at-home mother and homemaker. Now my twilight years usher in a new way of living. Now I have time to enjoy my growing family of grandchildren and great-grandchildren. I have time to bring the joy of painting back into my life, to see more of the wonders this world has to offer, and to read anything my heart desires and enjoy the company of family and friends.

A retired friend of mine who knew about my *oh-so-secret* experience during WWII recommended I read *The Forgotten 500* by Gregory Freeman, so I went to the library and checked it out. It was about the untold story of the OSS men who'd risked it all for one of the largest rescue missions of WWII. I was mesmerized by the story, learning what was going on behind the scenes. Just when the plot was coming to a dramatic climax, a memory flashed in my mind. I remembered a time I was right there in the OSS office, busy working at my desk, when the climactic event I was reading about in the book in my hands occurred. Suddenly it all fell into place! The light bulb came on.

I remember one day, a group of men in my office started shouting and cheering with frenzied excitement, barely able to contain themselves. Their enthusiasm was off the charts. Later that day, out of the office, I asked a close office friend, "What was going on in the office today?" He explained, "The rescue C-47 cargo plane was able to land on a runway the starving pilots had built. They all dropped their boots as they climbed into the plane." Those same words were in the book, explaining how hundreds of rescued American pilots who'd been hiding in Nazi-occupied Yugoslavia left their boots behind for the Serbian farmers and peasants who'd risked their lives to save them.

I learned so much from reading *The Forgotten 500*, and it opened my eyes to reveal secrets I never knew before. It was like discovering the secrets in someone's diary, and it inspired me to search for more answers. The OSS files had been locked away for fifty years, but in 1995, they were opened to the public. I found several other books in our local library that were written after the files were opened. The internet has also become an immense, invaluable resource. With all this information now at hand, my curiosity was set on fire, and I wanted to learn everything I could about my role in the OSS.

The Office of Strategic Services (OSS) was established in 1942. It grew very rapidly, and by 1944 the organization was desperate to find qualified help (the agency eventually hired around thirteen thousand personnel). The agency turned their focus to college students and college graduates, and thousands of positions opened for undercover help—anything from spying to office work. This was a revelation to me. I'd always wondered why I was immediately offered an important job in Washington, DC, when I'd only applied for a part-time summer job in Montgomery, Alabama.

When I was first introduced to my officemates, they'd frequently ask, "Did you have to go to 'The Farm' for training?" Of course, I'd needed no tactical training for keeping records in the procurement and supplies office, but now I was very curious about the "Farm" thing, so I did more research.

The OSS had several training sites. There was a one-hundred-acre area reaching over the Canadian border where our laws didn't apply. It was called "The Farm" by OSS insiders who were trained there. Officially, it was Code Area E, otherwise known as "Camp X." I've learned all the training areas had letter code names. That big, dilapidated building where I'd received my first assignment orders had been an old skating rink and was turned into an OSS orientational training area. Many US National Park areas were also used for military training. The Congressional Country Club had been the only dangerous "active" wartime OSS training area within the Washington, DC, city limits, however. That party I went to with a busload of other girls at the Congressional Country Club, and we danced and socialized with one hundred OSS men? Well, it turns out that night wasn't just a social event for those men who'd recently completed their training at "The Farm." It was, in fact, a final test to see if they'd break their cover and "tell all" with loose lips in a party kind of situation, especially if alcohol was involved.

I learned that code names were given to specialized training areas using two letters: "SO" = Special Operations; "UW" = Unconventional Warfare; and "MO" = Moral Operations. I was sending thousands of gallons of ink to code "MO" during WWII. I assumed at the time there must be lots of printing going on, and now, I know I assumed correctly. OSS operatives in China were printing instructional training materials. They also printed propaganda leaflets and fake ID cards and fake money to destabilize enemy governments. Buddy had told me he'd dropped propaganda leaflets by air when he was a navigator flying in the Pacific Theater, so it's highly likely they were printed by OSS agents using some of those gallons of ink I'd ordered and sent their way.

Of all the unusual code names, I was most curious about the code references to the famous Austrian-born movie star Hedy Lamarr. I'd often ordered "Hedy Lamarrs" and couldn't figure out what secret equipment they'd named after her. I learned in reading about the women of the OSS that she was more than a beautiful actress; she was a brilliant inventor. She co-invented the new OSS Hedy Lamarr Wireless Communication System, a radio guidance system for Allied forces' torpedoes. The OSS was busy inventing their own equipment during WWII. (There was even a big apartment complex named after Hedy Lamarr located across from our OSS headquarters on Navy Hill.) Interestingly enough, the radio frequency technology Hedy Lamarr co-invented with composer George Antheil laid the foundation for the Wi-Fi, GPS, and Bluetooth communication systems we use today.

"Joan-Eleanor" was another unusual code name. Two men invented two-way radio sets for the OSS agents to use in the field—a secretive type of telephonic communication system. They used their wives' combined first names, *Joan-Eleanor*, as the code name for their invention. I sent many of those units to Calcutta (Kolkata) to be flown "over the hump."

There were other code names I ordered that were explosive materials. "Black Joe" was a black substance that looked like coal, and "Aunt Jemima" was an explosive that looked like pancake mix. And, of course, those explosives could be molded into everyday items that no one would even suspect to be an explosive. Other deceptions were commonplace in the OSS realm—Monopoly games with hidden messages, pills that encased sensitive information, etc. "Matchbox" was code for a camera, and a "Fog Signal" was a small gadget resembling a nail that could wreck a train.

I recently learned about the forgotten CBI theater of WWII. At the time, the media wasn't very forthcoming with information concerning the war happening in China, Burma, and India. Many strategic roles were played by the OSS who were conducting unconventional clandestine projects in those countries during the war. I routinely sent equipment and supplies to China by way of Calcutta, India, and that always baffled me. I was young and uninformed, but now I understand a bit about why we were helping China. We had declared war on Japan after the Pearl Harbor attack on December 7th, 1941, but China was one of our Allies who'd been at war with Japan since 1937. I thought maybe China was at war with Japan too at the time, but I truly didn't know much about what was going on in the world outside my small piece of it.

I never knew anything about our director, "Wild Bill" Donovan, when I was in DC, but after reading about him, I knew more about his personality and leadership philosophy. He had the courage to write to President Franklin D. Roosevelt, suggesting that this country needed an agency like the Secret Intelligence Service (SIS) in Britain, also known as MI6. The two men soon became involved in the creation of the OSS early in 1942. Roosevelt called him his "idea man," but information about the OSS was never disclosed to the media. Donovan was never respected by our leading generals and admirals, and they avoided cooperating with any OSS projects. Wild Bill's philosophy said, "Workers need to have courage enough to break the rules." From everything I've heard, he *was* a wild man!

I look back now and realize what a truly unique experience I had working for the OSS. It was an extraordinary experience in a very unsettled time, and I feel honored to have been a part of it. I am proud of my role in supporting our boys and our government and helping protect our way of life.

CHAPTER 43

Whole, Content, and Unafraid

My spiritual quest has been a fulfilling journey, finely tuned in the simple solitude of my golden years. It's one of my favorite things, remembering my journey and realizing how differently it may have been without God by my side. I'm so thankful for His love, for His guiding in my life, and for the abundance of life He's given me.

Even though I was raised in a Christian household and believed in Jesus, it was a college assignment that truly ignited my deep curiosity about my religion and what I understood my relationship with God to be. In Sociology 101, we were given an assignment to write an essay on our philosophy of life, our beliefs about God, and our religious ideas. I wrote about the mysteries I didn't understand but also about the logical, realistic concepts of nature that make me *know* in my mind that there is a creator of this wonderful world. I wrote my personal perceptions about the universe, the Bible, and God.

I've always been totally aware that my brain can't factually *know* everything about God and His universe. Since I can't possibly know everything, I realize I need to have a strong, real, deeply held faith. I learn and wonder about the deeper meaning of what I have learned. I believe the human ability to *think* is one of the ways we most resemble God. This assignment in my college years made me go deeper than ever into what I did and did not believe and gave me a newfound appreciation for my faith. This personal spiritual renaissance was so profound that it has stayed with me until this day.

My culminating remark at the end of that sociology assignment was, "In my afterlife I believe my spirit will be given other interesting, challenging adventures and responsibilities in God's New World. I have never thought I'd be an angel simply floating around heaven for all eternity." The teacher gave me an A+ on my essay and asked me and another student to stand and read our papers to the class. I was nervous about exposing my deep, personal self to those impersonal classmates, including the one standing with me. I read my paper aloud, and then she arrogantly read hers. I wasn't surprised at all by her last remark: "This lifetime is all there is, and we should be having a lot of *wild* and *crazy fun*." I might've rolled my eyes a bit.

I was baptized when I was around twelve but never achieved a deeper faith until the sociology assignment made me delve into my innermost feelings and understandings. In college, there was a group of maybe a dozen girls along with two married women and their children, and we'd all meet in Montevallo for a "church service." It was a special time set aside for prayers, singing, and Bible study. Sometimes we'd have a guest speaker come from a big congregation in Birmingham to help us. Even though he was the only male present with a bunch of women and girls, he seemed glad to be there. This spiritual foundation, my faith, was an important part of my early life and has lifted me up and sustained me throughout.

God blessed me with my first grandchild, Laura, in 1975, and a new chapter opened in my life. There's something extraordinary about seeing, holding, and loving the children of your children. It truly is a circle of life. I wasn't expecting the pure joy that grandchildren can bring. I was smitten with little Laura. I called her "darling" pretty much all the time, but our favorite thing was when I called her "darling" and opened up my arms as she'd come running to me. When she began to talk, I realized she was saying something to me, and that was "narnie." Come to figure out, she was calling *me* "darling"! So I became Narnie to Laura and all the other grandchildren. And not only to the grandchildren, but my own children, their in-laws, friends, pretty much the whole family and extended family, and even some neighbors called me Narnie after that. It's something I've always cherished.

After Buddy passed away suddenly in 1998, my world was shattered, and it took quite some time for me to find my way again. After a while, a new lifestyle began to settle in, and I found a new appreciation for life in the most unexpected places.

My joy for singing was rekindled when my friend Pat King asked me to join the barbershop chorus she enjoyed. We had rehearsals and local performances, and we participated in competitive conventions in the US and Canada. I enjoyed several years of traveling with the chorus and hold many fond memories of those times.

Buddy never wanted to travel after his traumatic WWII years, so another new adventure for me was to start traveling with friends and family. I went on several spectacular trips and cruises, usually with friends or family in tow. I visited Israel with my office friend's family, and we drove through several European countries before returning home. My daughter, Bekah, and I went on a cruise to Russia and the Baltic Sea area. I went with my sister-in-law to Poland to visit Wieliczka. We saw one of the forty Auschwitz Jewish concentration camps and old salt mines. I went to Barcelona with a friend. And, at the youthful age of ninety-four, I flew with twelve other relatives for my granddaughter Sarah's wedding in London.

I still love to paint. You can often find me upstairs in my art studio, canvas and brush in hand. I painted the magnificent tourist attraction Leadenhall Market in London, where Sarah held her wedding reception. After that, I committed myself to painting a wedding or honeymoon picture for each of my six grandchildren.

I finally gave up driving at ninety-eight, but I still enjoy life in my comfortable home, nestled amid other historic houses along tree-lined streets. My little antique bungalow serves as a stopover for relatives and friends. Having company is always a real treat. I love reminiscing with others about times past, telling stories and sharing laughs together. These days I sit on my porch a lot, but my favorite time is on warm, relaxing summer days. I love the stillness, the peaceful solitude to think and meditate. With my morning cup of coffee in hand, I do my devotionals and revisit again and again the many golden memories accumulated over the years.

I don't like to be idle; I'd rather stay busy and keep my mind sharp. I try to stay active and walk around my block several times a week when the weather permits. I thank God for my health—for all my blessings—and I still attend church. I revel in the love and presence of God's steadfast Spirit in my heart. The real me is my unseen spirit, and I feel whole, content, and unafraid. My life is complete, and God has been good to me. Watching the children of my children and thinking of the generations that are here, and will be here, because of me and Buddy, I realize fully how life comes full circle. And life is good.

I have been a believer for as long as I can remember, but my spiritual formation has been refined over my lifetime. I have grown in my faith throughout the years, and now as I near a century of life on this earth, I can rest easy with my beliefs:

- I believe there is one God—the Spirit—who is the Creator of the universe, and all of nature on earth is a reflection of Him.
- I believe that Jesus is His Son who came to earth to light our way spiritually and to lead our journey to God, and He wants a relationship with us. Jesus died and overcame death to return to the Spirit of God.
- I believe that the Holy Spirit is a gift from God and is with us, helping us through this life, often in ways we don't understand.
- I believe God is living here in us and wants us to grow throughout our lives so we have a full and abundant life.

We grow closer to God through Jesus and His principles and teachings.

- I believe the church was established for us to have a supportive, compassionate, spiritual family here on earth as we travel the journey of life.

These aren't laws; they are my beliefs. I've lived in these beliefs, these principles, throughout my life, and God has blessed me greatly. I've had a very happy, good life filled with meaning and purpose—with a little adventure thrown in.

The End

Suggested Readings On the OSS and Its Part In World War II

The Forgotten 500: The Untold Story of the Men Who Risked All for the Greatest Rescue Mission of World War II, by Gregory A. Freeman

Wild Bill Donovan: The Spymaster Who Created the OSS and Modern American Espionage (A True Story of a WWII Spy), by Douglas Waller

Behind Japanese Lines: With the OSS in Burma, by Richard Dunlop

Sisterhood of Spies: The Women of the OSS, by Elizabeth P. McIntosh

A Man Called Intrepid: The Incredible WWII Narrative of the Hero Whose Spy Network and Secret Diplomacy Changed the Course of History, by William Stevenson

www.ingramcontent.com/pod-product-compliance
Lightning Source LLC
Chambersburg PA
CBHW060539160726
47991CB00001B/396